The Great Deluge:

A Yeats Bibliography

The Great Deluge:
A Yeats Bibliography

by
John E. Stoll

The Whitston Publishing Company
Incorporated
Troy, New York
1971

Library of Congress Catalog Card Number: 78-161084

ISBN 0-87875-010-X

Printed in the United States of America

Foreword

While the tides of Yeats scholarship generated over the past twenty years and beaten to a frenzy by the recent Centenary show signs of receding, they more than abundantly fulfill Allan Tate's prediction in 1942 of the deluge to come. We can never again return to the poetry with that feeling of pleasure and anticipation amounting to ignorant confidence and, of course, never with that "old nonchalance of the hand" that Yeats celebrated. As one who has read and appreciated him for at least fifteen years, I take this opportunity of paying tribute to the most compelling, most widely discussed, and greatest of contemporary poets in one of the few ways now tolerable. I do what remains to be "done," a bibliography, a pebble in the ocean of uncontrollable production. So I am put in the position of an Aherne, whether I want to be or not, and can never be like Robartes or the elder Statesman. There are no compensations, and were it not for the fact that Yeats's simplest poetry now seems to be the most slyly, most unscrupulously symbolic that I have ever encountered, I should be most unhappy.

John E. Stoll

For Yeats Scholars

Sing out the song; sing to the end, and sing
The strange reward of all that discipline.

EASILY ACCESSIBLE PRIMARY SOURCES

William Butler Yeats. *A Vision: A Reissue with the Author's Final Revisions*. New York: Macmillan, 1962.

-- *Essays and Introductions*. New York: Macmillan, 1961.

-- *Explorations*, selected by Mrs. Yeats. New York: Macmillan, 1962.

-- *John Sherman and Dhoya*, ed. Richard J. Finneran. Detroit: Wayne State, 1969.

-- *Letters on Poetry from W. B. Yeats to Dorothy Wellesley*. New York: Oxford, 1940.

-- *Letters to Katharine Tynan*, ed. Roger McHugh. New York: McMullen Books, 1953.

-- *Letters to the New Island*, ed. Horace Reynolds. Cambridge: Harvard, 1934.

-- *Mythologies*. New York: Macmillan, 1959.

-- *Selected Poems and Two Plays of William Butler Yeats,*

ed. M. L. Rosenthal. New York: Collier Books, 1967.

-- *The Autobiography of William Butler Yeats*. New York: Collier Books, 1969.

-- *The Collected Plays*. New York: Macmillan, 1953.

-- *The Collected Poems*. New York: Macmillan, 1952.

-- *The Collected Poems*. Definitive Edition, with the author's final revisions. New York: Macmillan, 1956.

-- *The Letters of W. B. Yeats*, ed. Allan Wade. New York: Macmillan, 1958.

-- *The Senate Speeches of W. B. Yeats*, ed. Donald R. Pearce. Bloomington: Indiana University Press, 1960.

-- *The Variorum Edition of the Plays of W. B. Yeats*, ed. Russell K. Alspach, assisted by Catharine Alspach. New York: Macmillan, 1966.

-- *The Variorum Edition of the Poems of W. B. Yeats*, ed. Peter Allt and Russell K. Alspach. New York: Macmillan, 1957.

-- *Uncollected Prose*, col. and ed. John P. Frayne. New York: Columbia University Press, 1970.

-- *W. B. Yeats and Sturge Moore: Their Correspondence*, ed. Ursula Bridge. London: Routledge and Paul, 1953.

-- John B. Yeats. *Letters to his Son W. B. Yeats and*

A Yeats Bibliography

    Others, ed. Joseph Hone. New York: E. P. Dutton,
    1946.

For a complete description of Yeats materials see Allan
Wade's *A Bibliography of the Writings of W. B. Yeats*,
third edition, rev. and ed. Russell K. Alspach. London:
Rupert Hart—Davis, 1968.

GENERAL CRITICAL BACKGROUND

Abrams, Meyer H. *The Mirror and the Lamp: Romantic Theory and the Critical Tradition.* New York: Norton, 1958.

Alvarez, A. *Stewards of Excellence: Studies in Modern British and American Poets.* New York: Scribner's, 1958.

Auden, W. H. *The Dyer's Hand.* New York: Random House, 1962.

-- *The Enchaféd Flood: The Romantic Iconography of the Sea.* New York: Random House, 1950.

Bayley, John. *The Romantic Survival.* Fair Lawn, New Jersey: Essential Books, 1957.

Blackmur, R. P. *Form and Value in Modern Poetry.* Garden City, New York: Anchor Books, 1957.

Bodkin, Maud. *Archetypal Patterns in Poetry.* New York: Vintage Books, 1958.

Bowra, C. M. *The Heritage of Symbolism.* New York: Macmillan, 1954.

A Yeats Bibliography

Bronowski, Jacob. *The Poet's Defence*. Cambridge, Eng—
    land: The University Press, 1939.

Brooks, Cleanth. *Modern Poetry and the Tradition*. Chapel
    Hill: University of North Carolina Press, 1939.

-- *The Well Wrought Urn*. New York: Harvest Books, 1947.

Bush, Douglas. *Mythology and the Romantic Tradition in
    English Poetry*. New York: Norton, 1963.

Common, Thomas. *Nietzsche as Critic, Philosopher, Poet
    and Prophet*. London: , 1901. A book Yeats read.

Daiches, David. *Poetry and the Modern World*. Chicago:
    University of Chicago Press, 1940.

Davidson, Donald. *Still Rebels, Still Yankees and Other
    Essays*. Baton Rouge: Louisiana State University
    Press, 1957.

Eliade, Mircea. *Myth and Reality*. New York: Harper and
    Row, 1963.

Eliot, T. S. *After Strange Gods*. New York: Harcourt, Brace,
    1933.

-- *On Poetry and Poets*. New York: Farrar, 1957.

Ellmann, Richard. *Eminent Domain: Yeats among Wilde,
    Joyce, Pound, Eliot, and Auden*. New York: Oxford
    Press, 1967.

-- , ed. *Edwardians and Late Victorians: English Institute Essays.* New York: Columbia University Press, 1960.

Fergusson, Francis. *The Idea of a Theater.* Princeton: Princeton University Press, 1949.

Harrison, John. *The Reactionaries: Yeats, Lewis, Pound, Eliot, Lawrence: A Study of the Anti—Democratic Intelligentsia.* New York: Schocken Books, 1967.

Holroyd, Stuart. *Emergence from Chaos.* Boston: Houghton Mifflin, 1957.

Hough, Graham. *Image and Experience.* Lincoln: University of Nebraska Press, 1955.

-- *The Last Romantics.* London: Dickworth, 1949.

Hyman, Stanley Edgar. *The Armed Vision.* New York: Vintage Books, 1955.

Kenner, Hugh. *Gnomon: Essays on Contemporary Literature.* New York: McDowell, Obolensky, 1958.

Kermode, Frank. *Romantic Image.* London: Routledge and Paul, 1957.

Langer, Susanne K. *Philosophy in a New Key.* New York: Mentor Books, 1952.

Leavis, F. R. *New Bearings in English Poetry.* Ann Arbor: University of Michigan Press, 1960.

MacLeish, Archibald. *Poetry and Experience.* Boston: Hough—
ton Mifflin, 1959.

MacNeice, Louis. *Modern Poetry.* New York: Oxford Press,
1938.

Matthiessen, F. O. *The Responsibilities of the Critic: Es—
says and Reviews.* New York: Oxford Press, 195?

Pinto, Vivian deSola. *Crisis in Modern Poetry.* New York:
Harper and Row, 1966.

Read, H. A. *A Coat of Many Colours.* London: Routledge
and Kegan Paul, 1945.

Richards, I. A. *Practical Criticism: A Study of Literary
Judgment.* New York: Harcourt, Brace, 1930.

-- *Science and Poetry.* London: Kegan Paul, 1935.

Spender, Stephen. *The Creative Element: A Study of Vision,
Despair and Orthodoxy among Some Modern Writers.*
London: Hamish Hamilton, 1953.

-- *The Destructive Element: A Study of Modern Writers
and Beliefs.* New York: Houghton Mifflin, 1936.

Tate, Allan. *Reactionary Essays on Poetry and Ideas.*
New York: Scribner's, 1936.

Tindall, William York. *Forces in Modern British Literature,
1885–1946.* New York: Knopf, 1947.

7

-- *The Literary Symbol.* Bloomington, Indiana: University of Indiana Press, 1955.

Whitehead, Alfred North. *Symbolism: Its Meaning and Effect.* New York: Capricorn Books, 1959.

Wilder, A. W. *The Spiritual Aspects of the New Poetry.* New York: Harper, 1940.

Wilson, Edmund. *Axel's Castle.* New York: Scribner's, 1959.

Comparative Studies or Studies placing the poems in an historical context are generally included under *Criticism and Biography: Books.*

ESOTERIC AND HISTORICAL BACKGROUND

Armstrong, A. H. *Plotinus.* London: Allen and Unwin, 1953.

Barker, Dudley. *Prominent Victorians.* New York: Atheneum, 1969.

Bayley, Harold. *The Lost Language of Symbolism.* London: Williams and Norgate, 1912.

Bergin, O. *Stories from Keating's History of Ireland.* Dublin: Hodges, Figgis, 1939.

Blau, J. L. *The Christian Interpretation of the Cabala in the Renaissance.* Port Washington, New York: Kennikat Press, 1944.

Blavatsky, Helena P. *Bulwer–Lytton's Novels and Isis Unveiled.* Cambridge: Harvard Press, 1957.

-- *The Key to Theosophy.* Point Loma California, 1923.

-- *The Secret Doctrine.* Pasadena, California: Theosophical University Press, 1952.

Boyd, E. A. *Ireland's Literary Renaissance*. London: Maunsel, 1916.

Burdett, Osbert. *The Beardsley Period*. London: John Lane, 1925.

Chadwick, H. M. *The Heroic Age*. Cambridge, England: The University Press, 1912.

Crowley, Aleister. *777 Revised; vel, Prolegomena Symbol—ica*. London: Neptune Press, 1955.

-- *The Spirit of Solitude: An Autobiography*. 2 vols. Lon—don, 1929.

Curtis, Edmund. *A History of Ireland*. London: Methuen, 1950.

Dalton, O. M. *Byzantine Art and Archaeology*. Oxford, Eng—land: Clarendon Press, 1923.

d'Alviella, Count Goblet. *The Migration of Symbols*. New York: University Books, 1956.

Dodds, E. R. *Proclus: The Elements of Theology*. Oxford: Oxford University Press, 1933.

Dunn, Joseph. *The Ancient Irish Epic Tale Tain Bo Cualange*. London, 1914.

Eglinton, John. *Literary Ideals in Ireland*. London: Fisher Unwin, 1899.

A Yeats Bibliography

Ellis—Fermor, Una Mary. *The Irish Dramatic Movement.*
London: Methuen, 1954.

Gregory, Lady Augusta. *Coole.* Dublin: Cula Press, 1931.

-- *Cuchulain of Muirthemne.* London: John Murray, 1902.

-- *Gods and Fighting Men.* London: John Murray, 1904.

-- *Lady Gregory's Journals,* ed. Lennox Robinson. New
York: Macmillan, 1947.

-- *Our Irish Theatre.* London: Putnam, 1914.

-- *Visions and Beliefs in the West of Ireland.* London:
Putnam, 1920.

Gwynn, Stephen. *Irish Literature and Drama.* London:
Nelson, 1936.

Hartmann, Franz. *The Life and Doctrines of Jacob Boehme.*
London: Kegan Paul, 1891.

Holmes, William G. *The Age of Justinian and Theodora.*
London: G. Bell, 1912.

Holt, Edgar. *Protest in Arms.* London: Putnam, 1960.

Hone, J. M. *The Poet in Contemporary Ireland.* Dublin and
London: Maunsel, 1916.

Hull, Eleanor. *The Cuchullin Saga in Irish Literature.*
London: , 1898.

Hyde, Douglas. *A Literary History of Ireland.* London: Fisher Unwin, 1910.

-- *The Story of Early Gaelic Literature.* London: Fisher Unwin 1922.

Jung, Carl Gustav. *Aion.* New York: Pantheon Books, 1959.

-- *Psychology and Alchemy.* Vol. 12 of *Collected Works,* ed. Read, Fadham, and Adler. New York: Pantheon Books, 1953.

Kingsford,   , and   Maitland. *The Perfect Way.* London: John M. Watkins, 1882.

Krans, Horatio Sheafe. *William Butler Yeats and the Irish Literary Revival.* New York: Haskell House, 1966.

Lang, Andrew, ed. *The Secret Commonwealth of Elves, Fauns, and Fairies.* London: D. Nutt, 1893.

Macardle, Dorothy. *The Irish Republic.* Dublin: Irish Press, 1957.

MacBride, Maud Gonne. *A Servant of the Queen.* Dublin: Golden Eagle Books, 1950.

MacKenna, Stephen. *Plotinus.* 5 vols. London: Warner, 1917–1930.

Maloney, William J. *The Forged Casement Diaries.* Dublin: Talbot Press, 1936.

Mathers, S. L. Mac Gregor. *The Kaballa Unveiled.* London: Kegan Paul, 1887.

Myers, F. W. H. *Human Personality and Its Survival of Bodily Death.* London: , 1907.

Noyes, Alfred. *The Accusing Ghost of Roger Casement.* London: Gollancz, 1957.

   Two Worlds for Memory. London: Sheed and Ward, 1953.

O'Grady, Standish. *Early Bardic Literature, Ireland.* London: Methuen (?), 1879.

   -- *Finn and His Companions.* London: Fisher Unwin, 1921.

   -- *History of Ireland.* London: Sampson, Low, Searle, Marston, etc., 1878–1880.

   -- *The Coming of Cuculain.* London: Methuen, 1894.

   -- *The Story of Ireland.* London: Methuen, 1894.

O'Leary, John. *Recollections of Fenians and Fenianism.* London: Downey and Co., 1896.

Pearse, P. H. *Three Lectures on Gaelic Topics.* Dublin: , 1898.

Regardie, Israel. *The Golden Dawn.* Chicago: Aries Press, 1937.

13

A Yeats Bibliography

-- *The Tree of Life.* London: , 1932.

Rice, Eugene F., Jr. *The Renaissance Idea of Wisdom.*
Cambridge: Harvard, 1958.

Robinson, Lennox, ed. *The Irish Theatre.* London: Mac—
millan, 1939.

Russell, George (A. E.). *Some Irish Essays.* Dublin:
Maunsel, 1906.

Ryan, Desmond. *The Rising.* Dublin: Golden Eagle Books,
1949.

Ryan, W. P. *The Irish Literary Revival.* London: Ward and
Donney, 1894.

Saurat, Denis. *Literature and the Occult Tradition.* New
York: Dial Press, 1930.

Scholem, Gershom G. *Major Trands in Jewish Mysticism.*
New York: Schocken Books, 1941.

-- *On The Kabbalah and Its Symbolism.* trans. Ralph
Manheim. New York: Schocken Books, 1965.

Senior, John. *The Way Down and Out: The Occult in
Symbolist Literature.* Ithaca, New York: Cornell
University Press, 1959.

Sharp, William (Fiona MacLeod). *The Dominion of Dreams.*
New York: Duffield, 1911.

A Yeats Bibliography

Sinnett, A. P. *Esoteric Buddhism.* London, 1885.

Thompson, William I. *The Imagination of an Insurrection.* New York: Oxford Press, 1967.

Tynan, Katherine. *The Middle Years.* Boston: Houghton Mifflin, 1917.

Von Hügel, Baron Friedrich. *The Mystical Element of Religion.* London: Dent, 1927.

Waite, Arthur E. *Brotherhood of the Rosy Cross.* London, 1924.

-- *The Book of Black Magic and of Poets.* Chicago: De Laurence, Scott and Co., 1910.

-- *The Hermetic and Alchemical Writings of Aureolus Philipus Theofrastus of Holenheim, Called Paracelsus the Great.* London: J. Elliott, 1894.

-- *The History of Magic.* New York: E. P. Dutton, 1940.

-- *The Pictorial Key to the Tarot.* New York: University Books, 1959.

Warnack, G. J. *English Philosophy Since 1900.* London: Oxford Press, 1958.

Watkins, Vernon. *The Lamp and the Veil.* London: Faber and Faber, 1946.

Wind, Edgar. *Pagan Mysteries in the Renaissance.* London:

Faber and Faber, 1958.

Yeats, John B. *Essays Irish and American*. Dublin: Talbot Press, and London: Fisher Unwin, 1918.

CRITICISM AND BIOGRAPHY: BOOKS

Adams, Hazard. *Blake and Yeats: The Contrary Vision.*
Ithaca, New York: Cornell University Press, 1955.

Allen, D. C., ed. *Four Poets on Poetry.* Baltimore: Johns
Hopkins University Press, 1959.

Bax, Clifford, ed. *Florence Farr, Bernard Shaw and W. B.
Yeats.* Dublin: Cuala Press, 1941.

Berryman, Charles. *W. B. Yeats: Design of Opposites.*
New York: Exposition Press, 1967.

Beum, Robert. *The Poetic Art of William Butler Yeats.*
New York: Frederick Unger, 1969.

Bjersky, Birgit. *Interpretations of the Cuchulain Legend in
the Works of W. B. Yeats.* Upsala: A.--B. Lundequistka
Bokhandlen, and Dublin: Hodges, Figgis, 1951.

Bloom, Robert. *Yeats.* New York: Oxford Press, 1970.

Bornstein, George. *Yeats and Shelley.* Chicago: University
of Chicago Press, 1970.

A Yeats Bibliography

Bradford, Curtis B. *Yeats at Work*. Carbondale, Illinois:
Southern Illinois University Press, 1965.

Brooks, Cleanth. *The Hidden God: Studies in Hemingway,
Faulkner, Yeats, Eliot, and Warren*. New Haven: Yale
University Press, 1963.

Bushrui, S. B. *Yeat's Verse—Plays: The Revisions 1900—
1910*. Oxford: Clarendon Press, 1965.

Cattui, Georges. *Trois Poëtes: Hopkins, Yeats, Eliot*.
Paris: Egloff, 1947.

Chatterjee, Bhabatosh. *The Poetry of W. B. Yeats*. Bombay:
Orient Longmans, 1962.

Clark, David R. *W. B. Yeats and the Theatre of Desolate
Reality*. Chester Springs, Pennsylvania: Dufour
Editions, 1965.

Davis, E. *Yeat's Early Contacts with French Poetry*.
University of South Africa, 1961.

Day—Lewis, Cecil. *Notable Images of Virtue: Emily Bronte,
George Meredith, W. B. Yeats*. Toronto: Ryerson Press,
1954.

Donoghue, Denis, ed. *The Integrity of Yeats*. Cork, Ireland:
Mercier Press, 1964.

-- and J. R. Mulryne, ed. *An Honoured Guest*. New York:
St. Martin's Press, 1966.

18

A Yeats Bibliography

Durkan, Michael J., ed. *W. B. Yeats, 1865–1965: A Catalogue of His Works and Associated Items in Olin Library*. Middletown, Connecticut: Wesleyan University
Library, 1965.

Durpee, Mary Ballard. *Words Alone Are Certain Good*. Dublin: Dolmen Press, 1961.

Ellmann, Richard. *Eminent Domain: Yeats Among Wilde,
Joyce, Pound, Eliot, and Auden*. New York: Oxford
Press, 1967.

-- *The Identity of Yeats*. New York: Oxford Press, 1954.

-- *Yeats: The Man and the Masks*. New York: Macmillan,
1948.

Engelberg, Edward. *The Vast Design: Patterns in W. B.
Yeat's Aesthetic*. Toronto: University of Toronto
Press, 1965.

Faulkner, Peter. *William Morris and W. B. Yeats*. Dublin:
Dolmen Press, 1962.

Fraser, George S. *W. B. Yeats*. New York: Longmans, 1962.

Garab, Arra M. *Beyond Byzantium: The Last Phase of
Yeats's Career*. DeKalb, Illinois: Northern Illinois
University Press, 1969.

Gibbon, Monk. *The Masterpiece and the Man: Yeats as I
Knew Him*. London: Hart–Davis, 1959.

19

Glenn, Charles Leslie. *Lonely Art: A Study of the Theme of Isolation in the Poetry of William Butler Yeats and Charles Baudelaire.* Cambridge: Harvard Press, 1959.

Gordon, D. J., ed., with contributions by Ian Fletcher, Frank Kermode, and Robin Skelton. *W. B. Yeats: Images of a Poet.* New York: Barnes and Noble, 1961.

Grossman, Allen R. *Poetic Knowledge in the Early Yeats: A Study of The Wind Among the Reeds.* Charlottesville, Virginia: University of Virginia Press, 1969.

Gurd, Patty. *The Early Poetry of W. B. Yeats.* Lancaster, Pennsylvania: Press of the New Era, 1916.

Gwynn, Stephen L., ed. *William Butler Yeats: Essays in Tribute.* Port Washington, New York: Kennikat Press, 1965.

Hall, James and Martin Steinmann, ed. *The Permanence of Yeats.* New York: Collier Books, 1950.

Henn, Thomas R. *The Lonely Tower.* New York: Barnes and Noble, 1966 (reissue).

-- *W. B. Yeats and the Poetry of War.* London: Oxford Press, 1967.

Hoare, Agnes D. *The Works of Morris and Yeats in Relation to Early Saga Literature.* Cambridge: Cambridge University Press, 1937.

Hoffman, Daniel. *Barbarous Knowledge in the Poetry of*

Yeats, Graves, and Muir. New York: Oxford Press, 1967.

Hone, Joseph. *W. B. Yeats, 1865–1939*. New York: St. Martin's Press, 1962 (reissue).

Jackson, Grace Emily. *Mysticism in A. E. and W. B. Yeats in Relation to Oriental and American Thought*. Columbus, Ohio: Ohio State University Press, 1932.

Jeffares, A. Norman. *A Commentary on the Collected Poetry of W. B. Yeats*. Stanford, California: University of Stanford Press, 1968.

-- *A Poet and a Theatre*. Groningen: Wolters, 1946.

-- *The Poems of W. B. Yeats: Studies in English Literature Number 4*. Great Neck, New York: Barron's Educational Series, 1961.

-- *W. B. Yeats: Man and Poet*. New Haven: Yale, 1949, and New York: Barnes and Noble, 1966 (reissue).

-- ,ed. *W. B. Yeats: Selected Criticism*. London: Macmillan, 1964.

-- , and K. G. W. Cross, ed. *In Excited Reverie: A Centenary Tribute to William Butler Yeats*. New York: Macmillan, 1965.

Jochum, K. *W. B. Yeats's Plays: An Annotated Checklist*. Saarbrucken: Institut der Universitat des Saarlandes, 1966.

Kirby, Sheelah. *The Yeats Country*. Dublin: Dolmen Press, 1962.

Koch, Vivienne. *W. B. Yeats: The Tragic Phase*. London: Routledge and Kegan Paul, 1951.

Lentricchia, Frank. *The Gaiety of Language: An Essay on the Radical Poetics of W. B. Yeats and Wallace Stevens*. Berkeley: University of California Press, 1968.

Levine, Bernard. *The Dissolving Image: The Spiritual—Esthetic Development of W. B. Yeats*. Detroit: Wayne State University Press, 1970.

Lucas, Frank L. *The Drama of Chekhov, Synge, Yeats, and Pirandello*. London: Cassell, 1963.

MacNeice, Louis. *The Poetry of W. B. Yeats*. London: Oxford Press, 1941, and Faber and Faber, 1967 (reissue).

Masefield, John. *Some Memories of W. B. Yeats*. New York: Macmillan, 1940.

Maxwell, D. E. S., and S. B. Bushrui, ed. *W. B. Yeats, 1865—1965: Centenary Essays*. Ibadan, Nigeria: Ibadan University Press, 1965.

Melchiori, Giorgio. *The Whole Mystery of Art: Pattern into Poetry in the Work of W. B. Yeats*. London: Routledge and Kegan Paul, 1960.

Menon, V. K. *The Development of William Butler Yeats.*
Edinburgh: Oliver and Boyd, 1960.

Miller, Joseph Hillis. *Poets of Reality: Six Twentieth–
Century Writers.* Cambridge: Belknap Press, 1965.

Miller, Liam, ed. *The Dolmen Press Yeats Centenary
Papers.* Chester Springs, Pennsylvania: Dufour
Editions, 1968.

Moore, Virginia. *The Unicorn: William Butler Yeats's
Search for Reality.* New York: Macmillan, 1954.

Nathan, Leonard E. *The Tragic Drama of William Butler
Yeats.* New York: Columbia University Press, 1965.

O'Donnell, J. P. *Sailing to Byzantium: A Study in the
Development of the Later Style and Symbolism in
the Poetry of William Butler Yeats.* Cambridge:
Harvard University Press, 1939.

Orel, Harold. *The Development of William Butler Yeats,
1885–1900.* Lawrence, Kansas: University of
Kansas Press, 1968.

Oshima, Shotaro. *W. B. Yeats and Japan.* Tokyo:
Hokuseido Press, 1965.

Parkinson, Thomas F. *W. B. Yeats, Self–Critic: A
Study of His Early Verse.* Berkeley: University of
California Press, 1951, and London: Faber and
Faber, 1967 (reissue).

-- *W. B. Yeats: The Later Poetry*. Berkeley: University of California Press, 1964.

Parrish, Stephen M., and James Allen Painter. *A Concordance to the Poetry of W. B. Yeats*. Ithaca, New York: Cornell University Press, 1963.

Perloff, Marjorie. *Rhyme and Meaning in the Poetry of Yeats*. The Hague: Mouton, 1970.

Pollock, John H. *William Butler Yeats*. London: Duckworth, and Dublin: Talbot Press, 1935.

Rajan, Balachandra. *W. B. Yeats: A Critical Introduction*. New York: Hillary House, and London: Hutchinson University Library, 1965.

Reid, Benjamin. *William Butler Yeats: The Lyric of Tragedy*. Norman, Oklahoma: University of Oklahoma Press, 1961.

Reid, Forest. *W. B. Yeats: A Critical Study*. London: Secker, 1915.

Romsley, Joseph. *Yeats's Autobiography: Life as Symbolic Pattern*. Cambridge: Harvard University Press, 1968.

Roth, William M., ed. *A Catalogue of English and American First Editions of William Butler Yeats*. New Haven: Yale University Press, 1939.

Rudd, Margaret. *Divided Image*. London: Routledge and

Kegan Paul, 1953.

Ryan, Sister Rosalie. *Symbolic Elements in the Plays of William Butler Yeats, 1892–1921*. Washington, D. C.: Catholic University Press, 1952.

Salvadori, Corinna. *Yeats and Castiglione: Poet and Courtier*. New York: Barnes and Noble, 1965.

Saul, George Brandon. *Prolegomena to the Study of Yeats's Poems*. Philadelphia: University of Pennsylvania Press, 1957.

-- *Stephens, Yeats, and Other Irish Concerns*. New York: New York Public Library, 1954.

-- *The Shadow of Three Queens*. Harrisburg, Pennsylvania: Stockpole, 1953.

Seiden, Morton. *The Poet as Mythmaker*. East Lansing, Michigan: Michigan State University Press, 1962.

Skelton, Robin, and Ann Saddlemyer, ed. *The World of W. B. Yeats: Essays in Perspective*. Distributed in the United States by the University of Washington Press, Seattle, 1965.

Smith, Arthur J. *Poet Young and Old: W. B. Yeats*. Toronto: University of Toronto Press, 1939.

Stallworthy, Jon. *Between the Lines: Yeats's Poetry in the Making*. Oxford: Clarendon Press, 1963.

25

A Yeats Bibliography

-- *Yeats: Last Poems; A Casebook.* London: Macmillan, 1968.

-- *Vision and Revision in Yeats's Last Poems.* Oxford: Clarendon Press, 1969.

Stauffer, Donald A. *The Golden Nightingale.* New York: Macmillan, 1949.

Steed, Christian K. *The New Poetic.* London: Hutchinson University Library, 1964.

Stock, Amy G. *W. B. Yeats: His Poetry and Thought.* Cambridge: Cambridge University Press, 1961.

Strong, L. A. G. *A Letter to W. B. Yeats.* London: Hogarth Press, 1934.

Tindall, William York. *W. B. Yeats.* New York: Columbia University Press, 1966.

Torchiana, Donald T. *W. B. Yeats and Georgian Ireland.* Evanston, Illinois: Northwestern University Press, 1966.

Ueda, Makoto. *Zeami, Bāsho, Yeats, Pound: A Study in Japanese and English Poets.* The Hague: Mouton, 1965.

Unterecker, John E. *A Reader's Guide to William Butler Yeats.* New York: Noonday Press, 1954.

-- , ed. *Yeats: A Collection of Critical Essays.*

A Yeats Bibliography

    Englewood Cliffs, New Jersey: Prentice—Hall, 1963.

Ure, Peter. *Towards a Mythology*. London: Hodder and
    Stoughton, 1946.

-- *W. B. Yeats*. New York: Grove Press, 1964.

-- *Yeats the Playwright*. New York: Barnes and Noble,
    1963.

Ussher, Arland. *Three Great Irishmen: Shaw, Yeats, Joyce.*
    London: Gollancz, 1952.

Veeder, William R. *W. B. Yeats: The Rhetoric of Repetition.*
    Berkeley: University of California Press, 1968.

Vendler, Helen H. *Yeats's Vision and the Later Plays*.
    Cambridge: Harvard University Press, 1963.

Wade, Allan. *A Bibliography of the Writings of W. B. Yeats.*
    3rd edition, rev. and ed. by Russell K. Alspach. Lon—
    don: Hart—Davis, 1968.

Walin, J., ed. *Interpretations*. London: Routledge, 1955.

Washburn, Priscilla. *Shaw, Rilke, Valéry and Yeats: The
    Domain of the Self*. New Brunswick, New Jersey:
    Rutgers University Press, 1964.

Whitaker, Thomas R. *Swan and Shadow*. Chapel Hill:
    University of North Carolina Press, 1964.

Wilson, F. A. C. *W. B. Yeats and Tradition*. London:

A Yeats Bibliography

    Gollancz, 1958.

  -- *Yeats's Iconography*. New York: Macmillan, 1960.

Winters, Yvor. *The Poetry of W. B. Yeats: The Swallow Pamphlets Number 10*. Denver: Alan Swallow, 1960.

Witt, Marion. *William Butler Yeats: English Institute Essays*. New York: Columbia University Press, 1947.

Wrenn, C. L. *W. B. Yeats: A Literary Study*. London: T. Murphy, 1916.

Wright, George T. *The Poet in the Poem: The Personae of Eliot, Yeats, and Pound*. Berkeley: University of California Press, 1962.

Yeats, John B. *Early Memories*. Dundrum: Cula Press, 1923.

Zwerdling, Alex. *Yeats and the Heroic Ideal*. New York: New York University Press, 1965.

ARTICLES

Adams, Hazard. "Some Yeatsian Versions of Comedy," *In Excited Reverie*, ed. Jeffares and Cross, pp. 152–170.

-- "Yeats, Dialectic, and Criticism," *Criticism*, X (1968), 185–199.

-- "Yeats Scholarship and Criticism: A Review of Research," *Texas Studies in Literature and Language*, III (1962), 439–451.

-- "Yeatsian Art and Mathematic Form," *The Centennial Review*, IV (1960), 70–88.

-- "Yeats's *Country of the Young*," *Publications of the Modern Language Association*, LXXII (1957), 510–519.

Adams, John F. " 'Leda and the Swan': The Aesthetics of Rape," *Bucknell Review*, XII (1964), 47–58.

Adams, Robert M. "Now That My Ladder's Gone--Yeats without Myth," *Accent*, XIII (1953), 140–152.

A Yeats Bibliography

Adkinson, R. V. "Criticizing Yeats," *Revue des Langues Vivantes*, XXXIII (1967), 423–430.

Adlard, John. "An Unnoticed Yeats Item," *Notes & Queries*, XVI (1969), 255.

Agarwala, D. C. "Yeats's Concept of Image," *Triveni*, July, 1967, 23–25.

Alexander, Jean. "Yeats and the Rhetoric of Defilement," *Review of English Literature*, VI (1965), 44–57.

Allen, James L., Jr. "Miraculous Birds, Another and the Same: Yeats's Golden Image and the Phoenix," *English Studies*, XLVIII (1967), 215–226.

-- "The Golden Bird on *The Golden Bough:* An Archetypal *Image* in Yeats's Byzantium Poems," *Diliman Review*, XI (1963), 168–221.

-- "William Butler Yeats's One Myth," *The Personalist*, XLV (1964), 524–532.

-- "Yeats's Bird–Soul Symbolism," *Twentieth Century Literature*, VI (1960), 117–122.

-- "Yeats' 'Her Vision in the Wood,' " *Explicator*, XVIII (1960), item 45.

-- "Yeats' 'A Long–Legged Fly,' " *Explicator*, XXI (1963), item 51.

-- "Yeats's Use of the Serious Pun, " *The Southern*

Quarterly, I (1963), 153–166.

Allt, G. D. P. "Yeats and the Revision of His Early Verse," *Hermathena*, LXIV (November, 1944).

-- "Yeats, Religion, and History," *Sewanee Review*, LX (1952), 624–658.

Alspach, Russell K. " 'It is Myself that I Remake," *James Joyce Quarterly*, III (1966), 95–108.

-- "Some Sources of Yeats's *The Wanderings of Oisin*," *Publications of the Modern Language Association*," LVIII (1943), 849–866.

-- "Some Textual Problems in Yeats," *Studies in Bibliography*, IX (1957), 51–67.

-- "The Variorum Edition of Yeats's Plays," *In Excited Reverie*, ed. Jeffares and Cross, pp. 194–206.

-- "Two Songs of Yeats," *Modern Language Notes*, LXI (1946), 395–400.

-- "Use by Yeats and Other Irish Writers of the Folklore of Patrick Kennedy," *Journal of American Folklore*, LIX (1946), 404–412.

-- "Yeats and Innisfree," *The Dolmen Press Centenary Papers*, ed. Liam Miller, pp. 69–84.

-- "Yeats's First Two Published Poems," *Modern Language Notes*, LVII (1943), 555–557.

A *Yeats Bibliography*

-- "Yeats's 'Maid Quiet,' " *Modern Language Notes,* LXV (1950), 252–253.

-- "Yeats's 'The Grey Rock,' " *Journal of American Folklore,* LXIII (1950), 57–71.

Alvarez, A. "Eliot and Yeats: Orthodoxy and Tradition," *Twentieth Century,* CLXII (1957), 149–163, 224–234.

Anon. "Books and Manuscripts of W. B. Yeats," London *Times Literary Supplement,* May 4, 1956, p. 276.

Anon. "From Sligo to Byzantium," London *Times Literary Supplement,* June 24, 1965, pp. 529–530.

Antippas, Andy P. "A Note on Yeats's 'Crazy Jane' Poems," *English Studies,* XLIX (1968), 557–559.

Atkins, Anselm. "The Vedantic Logic of Yeats' 'Crazy Jane,' " *Renascence,* XIX (1966), 37–40.

Auden, W. H. " 'In Memory of W. B. Yeats,' " *The Collected Poetry of W. H. Auden* (New York: Random House, 1945), pp. 48–51. See also *Yeats: A Collection of Critical Essays,* ed. John Unterecker, pp. 7–9.

-- "The Public v the Late Mr. W. B. Yeats," *The Partisan Reader* (New York: Dial Press, 1946), ed. William Phillips and Philip Rahv.

-- "Yeats as an Example," *Kenyon Review,* X (1948), 187–195. See also *The Permanence of Yeats,* ed. Hall and Steinmann, pp. 308–314.

-- "Yeats: Master of Diction," *Saturday Review of Literature*, XXVII (June 8, 1940), 14.

Ayling, Ronald. "W. B. Yeats on Plays and Players," *Modern Drama*, IX (1966), 1–10.

Baird, Sister Mary Julian. "A Play on the Death of God: The Irony of Yeats's *The Resurrection*," *Modern Drama*, X (1967), 79–86.

Baker, Howard. "Domes of Byzantium," *Southern Review*, VII (1942), 639–652.

Baksi, Promoti. "The Noh and the Yeatsian Synthesis," *Review of English Literature*, VI (1965), 34–43.

Barnes, T. R. "Yeats, Synge, Ibsen and Strindberg," *Scrutiny*, V (1937), 257–262.

Barnet, Sylvan. "W. B. Yeats and Brunetière on Drama," *Notes & Queries*, XVI (1969), 255–256.

Beach, Joseph Warren. "W. B. Yeats," *The Permanence of Yeats*, ed. Hall and Steinmann, pp. 195–199.

-- "Yeats and AE," *The Concept of Nature in the Nineteenth Century* (New York: Macmillan, 1936), pp. 535–538.

Becker, William. "The Mask Mocked: Or Farce and the Dialectic of Self," *Sewanee Review*, LXI (1953), 82–108.

A Yeats Bibliography

Beerbohm, Sir Max. "First Meeting with W. B. Yeats,"
    Atlantic, CC (September, 1957), 70–72.

Beja, Morris. "2001: Odyssey to Byzantium," *Extra-
    polation,* X (1969), 67–68.

Benson, C. "Yeats and Balzac's *Louis Lambert,*"
    Modern Philology, XLIX (1952).

  -- "Yeats's 'The Cat and the Moon,' " *Modern Lan-
    guage Notes,* LXVIII (1953), 220–223.

Bentley, Eric. "Yeats as a Playwright," *Kenyon Review,*
    X (1948), 196–208. See also *The Permanence of
    Yeats,* ed. Hall and Steinmann, pp. 213–223.

Berkelman, Robert. "The Poet, the Swan, and the Woman,"
    University of Kansas City Review, XXVIII (1962),
    229–230.

Beum, Robert. "Yeats the Rhymer," *Papers on English
    Language and Literature,* I (1965), 338–350.

  -- "Yeats's Idealized Speech," *Michigan Quarterly Re-
    view,* IV (1965), 227–233.

  -- "Yeats's Octaves," *Texas Studies in Literature and
    Language,* III (1962), 89–96.

Biderman, Sol. "Mount Abiegnor and the Maska: Occult
    Imagery in Yeats and Pessoa," *Luso–Brazilian Re-
    view,* V (1968), 59–74.

A Yeats Bibliography

Bierman, Robert. "Yeats' 'The Gyres,' " *Explicator*,
XIX (1961), item 44.

Blackmur, R. P. "Between Myth and Philosophy: Frag—
ments of W. B. Yeats," *Southern Review*, VII (1942),
407–425. See also *Yeats: A Collection of Critical
Essays*, ed. Unterecker, pp. 64–79.

-- "The Later Poetry of W. B. Yeats," *Southern Review*,
II (1936), 339–362. See also *The Permanence of
Yeats*, ed. Hall and Steinmann, pp. 38–59.

-- "Under a Major Poet," *American Mercury*, XXXI (1934),
244–246.

Blenner—Hassett, Roland. "Yeats' Use of Chaucer,"
Anglia, LXXII (1954), 455–462.

Block, Haskell M. "Flaubert, Yeats, and the National
Library," *Modern Language Notes*, LXVII (1952),
55–56.

-- "Yeats's *The King's Threshold:* The Poet and Soci—
ety," *Philological Quarterly*, XXXIV (1955), 206–218.

Bloom, E. A. "Yeats's' Second Coming,' " *University of
Kansas City Review*, XXI (1954), 103–110.

Bogan, Louise. " 'The Cutting of an Agate,' " *Nation*,
CXLVIII (February 25, 1939), 234–235.

Boland, Eavan. "Precepts of Art in Yeats's Poetry,"
Dublin Magazine, IV (1965), 8–13.

Boulger, James D. "Personality and Existence in Yeats," *Thought,* XXXIX (1964).

-- "Yeats and Irish Identity," *Thought,* XLII (1967), 185–213.

Boyd, E. A. "William Butler Yeats," *Portraits: Real and Imaginary* (New York: Doran, 1924), pp. 236–245.

Bradbrook, Muriel C. "Yeats and Elizabethan Love Poetry," *Dublin Magazine,* IV (1965), 40–55.

Bradford, Curtis B. "Discoveries: Second Series," *Massachusetts Review,* V (1964), 297–306.

-- "George Yeats: Poet's Wife," *Sewanee Review,* LXXVII (1969), 388–404.

-- "Journeys to Byzantium," *Virginia Quarterly,* XXV (1949), 205–225.

-- "Modern Ireland: An Address to American Audiences, 1932–1933," *Massachusetts Review,* V (1964), 256–268.

-- "The Order of Yeats's *Last Poems,*" *Modern Language Notes,* LXXVI (1961), 515–516.

-- "The Variorum Edition of Yeats's Poems," *Sewanee Review,* LXVI (1958), 668–678.

-- "Yeats and Maud Gonne," *Texas Studies in Literature and Language,* III (1962), 452–474.

A Yeats Bibliography

-- "Yeats's Byzantium Poems: A Study of Their Devel—
opment," *Publications of the Modern Language Association*, LXXV (1960), 110–125. See also *Yeats: A
Collection of Critical Essays*, ed. Unterecker, pp. 93–
130.

-- "*Yeats's Last Poems Again,*" *Yeats Centenary Papers*,
ed. Liam Miller, pp. 257–288.

Brian, John. "Hurt into Poetry: Some Recent Yeats Studies,"
Journal of General Education, XVIII (1967), 299–306.

Brogunier, Joseph. "Expiation in Yeats's Late Plays,"
Drama Survey, V (1966), 24–38.

Bromage, Mary C. "The Yeats—O'Casey Quarrel," *Michigan
Alumnus Quarterly*, LXIV (1958), 135–144.

Brooks, Cleanth. "Yeats: His Poetry and his Prose," *English* (London), XV (1965), 177–180.

-- "Yeats: The Poet as Myth—Maker," *Southern Review*,
IV (1938), 116–142. See also *The Permanence of Yeats*,
ed. Hall and Steinmann, pp. 60–84, and Brooks's *Modern
Poetry and the Tradition*, pp. 173–202.

Brown, Forman G. "Mr. Yeats and the Supernatural," *Sewanee
Review*, XXXIII (1925), 323–330.

Brown, T. J. "English Literary Autographs XLIX: William
Butler Yeats," *Book Collector*, XIII (1964), 53.

Burke, Kenneth. "On Motivation in Yeats," *Southern Review*,

VII (1942), 547—561. See also *The Permanence of Yeats,* ed. Hall and Steinmann, pp. 224—237.

-- "The Problem of the Intrinsic," *A Grammar of Motives* (New York: Prentice—Hall, 1945), pp. 465—484.

Bushrui, S. B. *"The Hour—Glass:* Yeats's Revisions, 1903—1922," *Centenary Essays,* ed. Maxwell and Bushrui, pp. 189—216.

-- *"The King's Threshold:* A Defence of Poetry," *Review of English Literature,* IV (1963), 81—94.

-- "Yeats's Arabic Interests," *In Excited Reverie,* ed. Jeffares and Cross, pp. 280—314.

Byars, John A. "Yeats's Introduction of the Heroic Types," *Modern Drama,* VIII (1966), 409—418.

Cambon, Glauco. "Yeats e la Lotta con Proten," *Aut Aut,* XXXVII (1957), 1—34.

Campbell, Harry M. "Yeats's 'Sailing to Byzantium,' " *Modern Language Notes,* LXX (1955), 585—589.

Carpenter, William M. "The *Green Helmet* Poems and Yeats's Myth of the Renaissance," *Modern Philology,* LXVII (1969), 50—59.

Cary, Elisabeth L. "Apostles of the New Drama," *Lamp,* XXVII (January, 1904), 593—598.

Cary, Richard. "William Butler Yeats at Colby College,"

A Yeats Bibliography

Colby Library Quarterly, Ser. VI (1964), pp. 360–369.

Caswell, Robert W. "Yeats' 'The Stolen Child,' " *Explicator*,
XXV (1967), item 64.

Cheadle, B. D. "Yeats and Symbolism," *English Studies
in Africa*, XII (1969), 132–150.

Chittick, V T. "Yeats the Dancer," *Dalhousie Review*,
XXXIX (1959), 333–348.

Christy, M. A. "Yeats's Teacher," London *Times Literary
Supplement*, May 20, 1965, p. 397.

Clark, David R. "Aubrey Beardsley's Drawings of the
'Shadows' in W. B. Yeats's *The Shadowy Waters*,"
Modern Drama, VII (1964), 267–272.

-- "Half the Characters had Eagles' Faces: W. B. Yeats'
Unpublished *Shadowy Waters*," *Massachusetts Review*,
VI (1964–1965), 151–180.

-- "Metaphors for Poetry: W. B. Yeats and the Occult,"
The World of W. B. Yeats: Essays in Perpective, ed.
Robin Skelton and Ann Saddlemyer, pp. 54–66.

-- "Nishikigi and Yeats's *The Dreaming of the Bones*,"
Modern Drama, VII (1964), 111–125.

-- "Poussin and Yeats's 'News for the Delphic Oracle,' "
Wascana Review, II (1967), 33–44.

-- "Vision and Revision in Yeats's *The Countess Cathleen*,"

Essays in Perspective, ed. Skelton and Saddlemyer, pp. 158–176.

-- "W. B. Yeats and the Drama of Vision," *Arizona Quarterly,* XX (1964), 127–141.

-- "Yeats and the Modern Theatre," *Threshold,* IV (1960), 36–56.

-- "W. B. Yeats's *Deirdre:* The Rigours of Logic," *Dublin Magazine,* XXXIII (1958), 13–21.

Clarke, Austin. "Glimpses of W. B. Yeats," *Shenandoah,* XVI (1965), 25–36.

-- "Yeats and LeFanu," London *Times Literary Supplement,* December 12, 1968, p. 1409.

Clemens, Katharine. "Some Recollections of William Butler Yeats," *Mark Twain Quarterly,* VI (1943), 17–18.

Clinton–Baddeley, V. C. "Reading Poetry with W. B. Yeats," *London Magazine,* IV (1957), 47–53.

Cohen, Joseph. "In Memory of W. B. Yeats--and Wilfred Owen," *Journal of English and Germanic Philology,* LVIII (1959), 637–649.

Coldwell, Joan. " 'Images that yet Fresh Images Beget': A Note on Book Covers," *Essays in Perspective,* ed. Skelton and Saddlemyer, pp. 152–157.

-- "The Art of Happy Desire: Yeats and the Little Maga—

zines," *Essays in Perspective,* ed. Skelton and Saddlemyer, pp. 40–53.

Cole, E. R. "Three Cycle Poems of Yeats and His Mystico-
Historical Thought," *The Personalist,* XLVI (1965), 73–80.

Colum, Padraic. "Mr. Yeats's Plays and Later Poems," *Yale
Review,* IV (1915), 381–385.

-- "Reminiscences of Yeats," *Tri–Quarterly* (Evanston,
Illinois), No. 4 (1965), pp. 71–76.

Comprone, Joseph J. "Unity of Being and W. B. Yeats' 'Under
Ben Bulben,' " *Ball State Forum,* XI, iii (1970), 41–49.

Condry, W. "A Hundred Years of *Walden,*" *Dublin Magazine,*
XXXI (1956), 42–46.

Conversi, Leonard. "Mann, Yeats, and the Truth of Art,"
Yale Review, LVI (1967), 506–523.

Cosman, Madeleine P. "Mannered Passion: W. B. Yeats and the
Ossianic Myths," *Western Humanities Review,* XIV (1960),
163–171.

Cowley, Malcolm. "The History of the Shee," *New Republic,*
CVIII (February 8, 1943), 185–186.

Crone, G. R. " ' Horseman, Pass By,' " *Notes & Queries,*
XVI (1969), 256–257.

Cronin, Anthony. "A Question of Modernity," *A Quarterly
Review,* I (1960), 283–292.

A Yeats Bibliography

Cross, K. G. W. "The Fascination of What's Difficult: A Survey of Yeats's Criticism and Research," *In Excited Reverie*, ed. Jeffares and Cross, pp. 315–337.

Daiches, David. "The Earlier Poems: Some Themes and Patterns," *In Excited Reverie*, ed. Jeffares and Cross, pp. 48–67.

-- "W. B. Yeats--I," *The Permanence of Yeats*, ed. Hall and Steinmann, pp. 106–124.

-- "W. B. Yeats--II," *Poetry and the Modern World*, pp. 156–189.

Davenport, A. "W. B. Yeats and the *Upanishads*," *Review of English Studies*, III (1952), 55–62.

Davidson, Donald. "Yeats and the Centaur," *Southern Review*, VII (1942), 510–516. See also *The Permanence of Yeats*, ed. Hall and Steinmann, pp. 250–256.

Davie, Donald. "*Michael Robartes and the Dancer*," *An Honoured Guest*, ed. Donoghue and Mulryne, pp. 73–87.

-- "Yeats and Pound," *Dublin Magazine*, XXX (1955), 17–21.

-- "Yeats, the Master of a Trade," *The Integrity of Yeats*, ed. Donoghue, pp. 59–70.

Day–Lewis, Cecil. "A Note on W. B. Yeats and the Aristocratic Tradition," *Essays in Tribute*, ed. Gwynn, pp. 157–182.

DeMan, Paul. "Symbolic Landscape in Wordsworth and Yeats,"

In Defense of Reading (New York: E. P. Dutton, 1962), ed. Brower and Poirier, pp. 22–37.

Desai, Rupin W. "A Note on 'Yeats on the Possibility of an English Drama,' " *Modern Drama*, XI (1969), 396–399.

Diskin, Patrick. "A Source for Yeats's ' The Black Tower,' " *Notes & Queries*, VIII (1961), 107 –108.

Donaldson, A. "A Note on W. B. Yeats' 'Sailing to Byzantium,' " *Notes & Queries*, I (1954), 34–35.

Donoghue, Denis. "Introduction," *The Integrity of Yeats*, ed. Denis Donoghue, pp. 9–20.

-- "On *The Winding Stair*," *An Honoured Guest*, ed. Donoghue and Mulryne, pp. 106–123.

-- "The Vigour of Its Blood: Yeats's *Words for Music Perhaps*, " *Kenyon Review*, XXI (1959), 376–387.

-- "Tradition, Poetry, and W. B. Yeats," *Sewanee Review*, LXIX (1961), 476–484.

-- "Yeats and the Clean Outline," *Sewanee Review*, LXV (1957), 202–225.

Downes, Gwladys V. "W. B. Yeats and the Tarot," *Sewanee Review*, LXV (1957), 202–225.

Drew, Elizabeth, and John L. Sweeney. "W. B. Yeats," *Directions in Modern Poetry* (New York: Norton, 1940), pp. 148–171.

A Yeats Bibliography

Dume, T. L. "Yeats' Golden Tree and Birds," *Modern Language Notes*, LXVIII (1952), 404–407.

Dunsany, Lord. "Four Poets: AE, Kipling, Yeats, Stephens," *Atlantic*, CCI (April, 1958), 77–80.

Dunseath, T. R. "Yeats and the Genesis of Supernatural Song," *English Literary History*, XXVIII (1961), 399–416.

Edwards, O. "Yeats's 'The Fisherman,' " *Wales*, VII, 222–223.

Edwards, Philip. " Yeats and the Trinity Chair," *Hermathena*, CI (1965), 5–12.

Eglinton, John. "Mr. Yeats's *Autobiographies*," *Dial*, LXXXIII (August, 1927), 94–97.

-- "Yeats and His Story," *Irish Literary Portraits* (London: Macmillan, 1935), pp. 17–38.

Eliot, T. S. "The Poetry of W. B. Yeats," *Southern Review*, VII (1942), 442–454. See also *The Permanence of Yeats*, ed. Hall and Steinmann, pp. 296–307, and *Yeats: A Collection of Critical Essays*, ed. Unterecker, pp. 54–63.

-- "Ulysses, Order, and Myth," *Dial*, LXXV (November, 1923), 480–483.

Ellmann, Richard. "Eliot's Conversion," *Tri–Quarterly* (Evanston, Illinois), No. 4 (1965), pp. 77–80.

-- "Ez and Old Billum, " *Kenyon Review*, XXVIII (1966), 470–495.

-- "Joyce and Yeats," *Kenyon Review*, XII (1950), 618–638.

-- "Reality," *Yeats: A Collection of Critical Essays*, ed. Unterecker, pp. 163–174. See also Ellmann's *The Man and the Masks*, pp. 273–286.

-- "Robartes and Aherne: Two Sides of a Penny," *Kenyon Review*, X (1948), 177–186.

-- "The Art of Yeats: Affirmative Capability," *Kenyon Review*, XV (1953), 357–385.

-- "Yeats and Eliot," *Encounter*, XXV (1965), 53–55.

-- "Yeats and Joyce," *Yeats Centenary Papers*, ed. Liam Miller, pp. 447–477.

-- "Yeats Without Analogue," *Kenyon Review*, XXVI (1964), 30–47.

Empson, William. "The Variants for the Byzantium Poems," *Essays Presented to Amy Stock*, pp. 111–136. See also *Phoenix* (Korea), X (1965), 1–26.

-- "Mr. Wilson on the Byzantium Poems," *Review of English Literature*, I (1960), 51–56.

Emslie, MacDonald. "Gestures in Scorn of an Audience," *Centenary Essays*, ed. Maxwell and Bushrui, pp. 102–126.

Engelberg, Edward. " 'He Too Was in Arcadia': Yeats and the Paradox of the Fortunate Fall," *In Excited Reverie*, ed. Jeffares and Cross, pp. 69–92.

A Yeats Bibliography

-- "Passionate Reverie: W. B. Yeats's Tragic Correlative," *Toronto Quarterly*, XXI (1962), 201–222.

-- "Picture and Gesture in the Yeatsian Aesthetic," *Criticism*, III (1961), 101–120.

-- "The New Generation and the Acceptance of Yeats," *Centenary Essays*, ed. Maxwell and Bushrui, pp. 88–101.

Fackler, Herbert V. "W. B. Yeats' *Deirdre:* Intensity by Condensation," *Forum* (Houston), VI, iii (1968), 43–46.

Fallon, Gabriel. "Profiles of a Poet," *Modern Drama*, VII (1964), 329–344.

Farag, Fahmy Fawsy. "Oriental and Celtic Elements in the Poetry of W. B. Yeats," *Centenary Essays*, ed. Maxwell and Bushrui, pp. 33–53.

-- "The Unpopular Theatre of W. B. Yeats," *Cairo Studies in English*, 1963–1966, pp. 97–108.

-- "W. B. Yeats's Daimon," *Cairo Studies in English*, 1961–1962, pp. 135–144.

Faulkner, Peter. "Yeats and the Irish Eighteenth Century," *Yeats Centenary Papers*, ed. Liam Miller, pp. 109–124.

-- "Yeats as Critic," *Criticism*, IV (1962), 328–339.

-- "Yeats, Ireland, and Ezra Pound," *Threshold*, VII (1963), 58–68.

-- "W. B. Yeats and William Morris," *Threshold,* IV (1960), 18–27.

Fay, W. G. "The Poet and the Actor," *Essays in Tribute,* ed. Gwynn, pp. 115–134.

Fay, William P. "A Yeats Centenary," *Tri–Quarterly,* No. 4 (1965), pp. 68–70.

Fixler, Michael. "The Affinities between J.–K. Huysmans and the 'Rosicrucian' Stories of W. B. Yeats," *Publications of the Modern Language Association,* LXXIV (1959), 464–469.

Flanagan, Thomas. "A Discourse by Swift, a Play by Yeats," *University Review* (Dublin), V (1968), 9–22.

Flannery, James W. "Action and Reaction at the Dublin Theatre Festival," *Educational Theatre Journal,* XIX (1967), 72–80.

Fletcher, Ian. "History and Vision in the Work of W. B. Yeats," *Southern Review,* IV (1968), 105–126.

-- "Leda and St. Anne," *Listener,* LVII (1957), 305–307.

-- "Rhythm and Pattern in *Autobiographies,*" *An Honoured Guest,* ed. Donoghue and Mulryne, pp. 165–189.

-- "Yeats and Lissadell," *Centenary Essays,* ed. Maxwell and Bushrui, pp. 62–78.

Fraser, G. S. "A Yeats Borrowing," London *Times Literary*

Supplement, February 25, 1965, p. 156.

-- "W. B. Yeats and T. S. Eliot," *T. S. Eliot: A Symposium* (New York: Farrar, 1958), ed. Neville Braybrooke, pp. 196–216.

-- "Yeats as a Philosopher," *Phoenix* (Korea), X (1965), 46–59. Yeats issue.

-- "Yeats's 'Byzantium,' " *Critical Quarterly,* II (1960), 253–261.

Fréchet, René. "Le centenaire de Yeats," *Études Anglaises,* XVIII (1965), 225–227.

-- "L'étude de Yeats: Textes, jugements, et éclaircisse –ments," *Études Anglaisses,* XIV (1961), 36–47.

-- "Yeats's 'Sailing to Byzantium' and Keats's 'Ode to a Nightingale,' " *Centenary Essays,* ed. Maxwell and Bushrui, pp. 217–219.

Frye, Northrop. "The Rising of the Moon: A Study of *A Vision,*" *An Honoured Guest,* ed. Donoghue and Mul–ryne, pp. 8–33.

-- "The Top of the Tower: A Study of the Imagery of Yeats," *Southern Review,* V (1969), 850–871.

-- "Yeats and the Language of Symbolism," *Toronto Quar–terly,* XVII (1947), 1–17.

Fullwood, Daphne. "Balzac and Yeats," *Southern Review,*

V (1969), 935–949.

Garab, Arra M. "Fabulous Artifice: Yeats's 'Three Bushes' Sequence," *Criticism*, VII (1965), 235–249.

-- "Times of Glory: Yeats's 'The Municipal Art Gallery Revisited,' " *Arizona Quarterly*, XXI (1965), 243–254.

-- "Yeats and *The Forged Casement Diaries*," *English Language Notes*, II (1965), 289–292.

-- "Yeats's 'Dark Between the Polecat and the Owl,' " *English Language Notes*, II (1965), 218–220.

Gaskell, Ronald. " ' Purgatory,' " *Modern Drama*, IV (1962), 397–401.

Geckle, George L. "Stephen Dedalus and W. B. Yeats: The Making of the Villanelle," *Modern Fiction Studies*, XV (1969), 87–96.

Gerstenberger, Donna. "The Saint and the Circle: The Dramatic Potential of an Image," *Criticism*, II (1960), 336–341.

-- "Yeats and Synge: 'A Young Man's Ghost.' " *Centenary Essays*, ed. Maxwell and Bushrui, pp. 79–87.

-- "Yeats and the Theater: A Selected Bibliography," *Modern Drama*, VI (1963), 64–71.

Gil, Kim Jong. "The Topography of Yeats's Poetry," *Phoenix* (Korea), X (1965), 84–95. Yeats issue.

A Yeats Bibliography

Gilomen, Walter. "George Moore and his Friendship with W. B. Yeats," *English Studies*, XIX (1936), 116–120.

Glasheen, Adaline. "Joyce and Yeats," *A Wake Newsletter*, IV (1967), 30.

Gleckner, Robert F. "Blake and Yeats," *Notes & Queries*, II (1955), 38.

Glen, Heather. "The Greatness of Yeats's *Meditations*," *The Critical Review*, XII (1969), 29–44.

Glick, Wendell. "Yeats's Early Reading of *Walden*," *Boston Public Library Quarterly*, V (1953), 164–166.

Glicksberg, Charles. "William Butler Yeats and the Hatred of Science," *Prairie Schooner*, XXVIII (1953), 29–36.

-- "W. B. Yeats and the Role of the Poet," *Arizona Quarterly*, IX (1953), 293–307.

Goldgar, Harry. "Axël de Villiers de I'Isle—Adam et *The Shadowy Waters* de W. B. Yeats," *Revue de Litt. Comparee*, XXIV (1950), 563–574.

-- "Note sur la Poésie de William Butler Yeats," *Le Bayou*, No. 2 (1958), pp. 547–552.

-- "Yeats and the Black Centaur in France," *Western Humanities Review*, XV (1961), 111–122.

Goldzung, Valerie J. "Yeats's Tradition and 'The Song of Wandering Aengus,' " *Massachusetts Studies in English*,

I (1967), 8–16.

Gonne, Maud. "Yeats and Ireland," *Essays in Tribute*, ed. Gwynn, pp. 15–34.

Goodwin, K. L. "Some Corrections to Standard Biographies of Yeats," *Notes & Queries*, XII (1965), 260–262.

Gordon, D. J. , and Ian Fletcher. "Byzantium," *Images of a Poet*, ed. Gordon, pp. 81-90.

-- "The Poet and the Theatre," *Images of a Poet*, ed. Gordon, pp. 56–80.

Gose, Eliott B., Jr. "The Lyric and the Philosophic in Yeats' *Calvary*," *Modern Drama*, II (1959–1960), 370–376.

Greene, D. J. "Yeats's Byzantium and Johnson's Lichfield," *Philological Quarterly*, XXXIII (1954), 433–435.

Gregory, Horace. "W. B. Yeats and the Mask of Jonathan Swift," *Southern Review*, VII (1942), 492–509.

Grierson, H. "Fairies--from Shakespeare to Mr. Yeats," *Dublin Review*, CXLVIII, 271–284, 297.

Gross, Martha. "Yeats' 'I am of Ireland,' " *Explicator*, XVII (1958), item 14.

Guha, Naresh. "Discovery of a Modern Indian Poet," *A Quarterly of South Asian Literature* (University of Chicago), III (1966), 58–73.

Gullans, Charles B. " 'Leda and the Swan,' " London *Times Literary Supplement*, November 16, 1962, p. 873.

Guthrie, W. N. "W. B. Yeats," *Sewanee Review*, IX (1901), 328–331.

Gwynn, Frederick L. "Yeats's Byzantium and Its Sources," *Philological Quarterly*, XXXII (1953), 9–21.

Gwynn, Stephen L. "Scattering Branches," *Essays in Tribute*, ed. S. L. Gwynn, pp. 1–14.

-- "The Passing of W. B. Yeats," *Fortnightly Review*, LXXXV (March, 1939), 347–349.

-- "Yeats's Poetry and Work," *Fortnightly Review*, CXXXVIII (August, 1935), 234–238.

Haerdter, Michael. "William Butler Yeats--Irisches Theater Zwischen Symbolismus und Expressionismus," *Maske und Kothurn*, XI (1965), 30–42.

Hahn, Sister M. Norma. "Yeats's 'The Wild Swans at Coole': Meaning and Structure," *College English*, XXII (1961), 419–421.

Hall, James, and Martin Steinmann. "The Seven Sacred Trances," *The Permanence of Yeats*, ed. Hall and Steinmann, pp. 1–8.

Halloran, William F. "W. B. Yeats and William Sharp: The Archer Vision," *English Language Notes*, VI (1969), 273–280.

Hamard, Jean. "Byzantium de W. B. Yeats," *Les Langues Modernes*, LX (1966), 54–63.

Harper, George Mills. " 'All the Instruments Agree': Some Observations on Recent Yeats Criticism," *Sewanee Review*, LXXIV (1966), 739–754.

-- "Yeats's Intellectual Nationalism," *Dublin Magazino*, IV, ii (1965), 8–21. Yeats Centenary Edition.

-- "Yeats's Quest for Eden," *Yeats Centenary Papers*, ed. Liam Miller, pp. 289–332.

Harris, Wendell. "Innocent Decadence: The Poetry of the *Savoy*," *Publications of the Modern Language Association*, LXXVII (1962), 629–636.

Harvey, W. J. "Visions and Revisions," *Essays in Criticiam*, IX (1959), 287–299.

Häusermann, H. W. "W. B. Yeats and W. J. Turner, 1935–1937 (with Unpublished Letters)," *English Studies*, XL (1959), 233–241.

-- "W. B. Yeats and W. J. Turner, 1935–1937 (with Unpublished Letters)," *English Studies*, XLI (1960), 241–253.

-- "W. B. Yeats's Criticism of Ezra Pound," *Sewanee Review*, LVII (1949), 437–455.

Haydn, Hiram. "The Last of the Romantics: An Interpretation to the Symbolism of William Butler Yeats," *Sewanee Review*, LV (1947), 297–323.

A Yeats Bibliography

Healy, J. V. "Yeats and His Imagination," *Sewanee Review*, LIV (1946), 650–659.

Henderson, Philip. "Politics and W. B. Yeats," *The Poet and Society* (London: Secker and Warburg, 1939), pp. 132–153.

Henn, T. R. "Moore and Yeats," *Dublin Magazine*, IV, ii (1965), 63–77. Yeats Centenary Edition.

-- "The Accent of Yeats' *Last Poems*," *Essays and Studies*, IX (1956), 56–72.

-- "*The Green Helmet* and *Responsibilities*," *An Honoured Guest*, ed. Donoghue and Mulryne, pp. 34–53.

-- "The Rhetoric of Yeats," *In Excited Reverie*, ed. Jeffares and Cross, pp. 102–122.

-- "Toward the Values," *Southern Review*, V (1969), 833–849.

-- "W. B. Yeats and the Irish Background," *Yale Review*, XLII (1953), 351–364.

-- "Yeats and the Picture Galleries," *Southern Review*, I (1965), 57–75.

-- "W. B. Yeats and the Poetry of War," *Proceedings of the British Academy*, LI (1965), 301–319.

-- "Yeats' Symbolism," *The Integrity of Yeats*, ed. Donoghue, pp. 33–46.

Herlitschka, Herbert E., trans. "Die Gesetzestafeln,"
Antaios, I (1959), 367–378.

Hethmon, Robert H. "Total Theatre and Yeats," *Colorado Quarterly*, XV (1967), 361–377.

Higgins, F. R. "Yeats as Irish Poet," *Essays in Tribute*, ed. Gwynn, pp. 145–156.

Hill, Douglas. "Yeats and the Invisible People of Ireland," *Brigham Young University Studies*, VII (1965), 61–67.

Hodges, Robert R. "The Irony of Yeats's 'Long–Legged Fly,' " *Twentieth Century Literature*, XII (1966), 27–30.

Hoffman, Christine B. "William Butler Yeats and the Nobel Prize," *The Personalist*, XLIX (1968), 103–115.

Holloway, John. "Style and the World in *The Tower*," *An Honoured Guest*, ed. Donoghue and Mulryne, pp. 88–105.

-- "Yeats and the Penal Age," *Critical Quarterly*, VIII (1966), 58–66.

Hone, J. M. "Yeats as Political Philosopher," *London Mercury*, XXXIX, 492–496.

Houghton, Walter E. "Yeats and Crazy Jane: The Hero in Old Age," *Modern Philology*, XL (1943), 316–329. See also *The Permanence of Yeats*, ed. Hall and Steinmann, pp. 327–348.

Howarth, Herbert. "Whitman and the Irish Writers," *Comparative*

Literature, XII (1960), 479–488.

-- "Yeats: The Variety of Greatness," *Western Humanities Review,* XIX (1965), 335–343.

Hubbell, Lindley W. "Yeats, Pound, and Nō Drama," *East–West Review,* I (1964), 70–78.

Hurwitz, Harold M. "Yeats and Tagore," *Comparative Literature,* XVI (1964), 55–64.

Hutchins, Patricia. "Yeats and Pound in England," *Texas Quarterly,* IV (1961), 203–216.

Ishibashi, Hiro. "Yeats and the Noh: Types of Japanese Beauty and their Reflection in Yeats's Plays," *Yeats Centenary Papers,* ed. Liam Miller, pp. 125–196.

Ishkandar, Fayez. "Yeats and Cocteau: Two Anti–Romanticists," *Cairo Studies in English,* 1963–1966, pp. 119–135.

J., C. R. "Yeats's 'The Wild Swans at Coole,' " *Explicator,* II (1944), item 4.

Jablonski, W. M. "Bemerkenswertes aus dem Leben und der Gedaukwelt des Irischen Dichtes William Butler Yeats," *Robert Boehringer: Eine Freundgesabe* (Tubingen: Mohr, 1957), ed. Erich and Wilhelm Hoffman, pp. 325–329.

Jacobs, Edward C. "Yeats and the Artistic Epiphany," *Discourse,* XII (1969), 292–305.

Jarrell, Randall. "The Development of Yeats's Sense of Real–

ity," *Southern Review*, VII (1942), 653–666.

Jeffares, A. Norman. "An Account of Recent Yeatsiana," *Hermathena*, LXXII (1948), 21–43.

-- "John Butler Yeats," *Dublin Magazine*, IV, ii (1965), 30–37. Yeats issue.

-- "Notes on Yeats's Fragments," *Notes & Queries*, CXIV (1948), 488–491.

-- "Notes on Yeats's 'Lapis Lazuli,' " *Modern Language Notes*, LXV (1950), 488.

-- "Poet's Tower," *Envoy*, V (1951), 45–55.

-- "The Byzantine Poems of W. B. Yeats," *Review of English Studies*, XXII (1946), 44–52.

-- "The Byzantine Poems of W. B. Yeats," *Revue des Langues Vivantes*, XXXI (1965), 353–359.

-- "The Criticism of Yeats," *Phoenix* (Korea), X (1965), 27–45.

-- " 'The New Faces': A New Explanation," *Review of English Studies*, XXIII (1947), 349–353 .

-- "The Sources of Yeats's 'A Meditation in Time of Civil War,' " *Notes & Queries*, CXCIII (1948), 522.

-- "The Yeats Country," *Modern Language Quarterly*, XXV (1964), 218–222.

-- "Thor Ballylee," *English Studies*, XXVIII (1948), 161–168.

-- "Two Songs of a Fool and Their Explanation," *English Studies*, XXVI (1945), 169–171.

-- "Yeats as a Modern Poet," *Mosaic*, II (1969), 53–58.

-- "Yeats as Critic," *English*, XV (1965), 173–176.

-- "W. B. Yeats and His Method of Writing Verse," *The Nineteenth Century and After*, CXXXIX (March, 1946), 123–128. See also *The Permanence of Yeats*, ed. Hall and Steinmann, pp. 270–276.

-- "Yeats the Public Man," *The Integrity of Yeats*, ed. Donoghue, pp. 21–32.

-- "Yeats's Byzantine Poems and the Critics," *English Studies in Africa*, V (1962), 11–28.

-- "Yeats's 'The Gyres': Sources and Symbolism," *Huntington Library Quarterly*, XV (1951), 89–97.

Jensen, Ejner. "The Antinomical Vision of W. B. Yeats," *Xavier University Studies*, III (1964), 127–145.

Johnston, Charles. "The Theosophical Movement," *Theosophical Quarterly*, V (1907), 16–26.

-- "The Variorum Yeats," *Tamarack Review*, XI, 97–102.

Jones, James L. "Keats and Yeats: 'Artificers of the Great

Moment,' " *Xavier University Studies*, IV (1965), 125–150.

Jumper, William C. "Form versus Structure in a Poem of W. B. Yeats," *Iowa English Yearbook*, No. 7 (1962), pp. 41–44.

Kain, R. M. "Yeats and Irish Nationalism," *Centenary Essays*, ed. Maxwell and Bushrui, pp. 54–61.

Kantak, V. Y. "Yeats's Indian Experience," *Indian Journal of English Studies*, VI (1965), 80–101.

Kayser, Wolfgang. "W. B. Yeats: Der dichterische Symbol— ismus übersetzt und erläutert," *Gestaltung—Umgestaltung* (Leipzig: Koehler and Amelang, 1957), ed. Joachim Miller, pp. 239–248.

Keith, W. J. "Yeats's Arthurian Black Tower," *Modern Lan— guage Notes*, LXXV (1960), 119–123.

-- "Yeats's 'The Empty Cup,' " *English Language Notes*, IV (1967), 206–210.

Kelleher, John V. "Yeats's Use of Irish Materials," *Tri— Quarterly*, No. 4 (1965), pp. 115–125.

Kennelly, Brendan. "The Heroic Ideal in Yeats's Cuchulain Plays," *Hermathena*, CI (1965), 13–21. Yeats issue.

Kenner, Hugh. "The Sacred Book of the Arts," *Sewanee Review*, LXIV (1956), 574–590. See also Kenner's *Gnomon*, pp. 9–29, and *Yeats: A Collection of Critical Essays*, ed. Unterecker, pp. 10–22.

Kermode, Frank. "Players and Painted Stage," *The Integrity of Yeats*, ed. Donoghue, pp. 47–57.

-- "The Artist in Isolation," *Yeats: A Collection of Critical Essays*, ed. Unterecker, pp. 37–42. See also Kermode's *Romantic Image*.

-- "The Dancer," *Images of a Poet*, ed. Gordon, pp. 120–128.

-- "The New Apocalyptists," *Partisan Review*, XXXIII (1966), 339–361.

Kersnowski, Frank L. "Portrayal of the Hero in Yeats's Poetic Drama," *Renascence*, XVIII (1965), 9–15.

Khanna, Urmilla. "The Tower Symbol in the Poetry of Yeats," *An English Miscellany* (India), III (1965), 9–18.

Killen, A. M. "Some French Influences in . . . W. B. Yeats . . .," *Comparative Literature*, VIII (1956), 1–8.

King, B. A. "Yeats's Irishry Prose," *Centenary Essays*, ed. Maxwell and Bushrui, pp. 127–136.

Kleinstück, Johannes. "William Butler Yeats: *At the Hawk's Well*," *Das Moderne Englische Drama: Interpretationem* (Berlin: Erich Schmidt, 1963), ed. Horst Oppel, pp. 149–165.

-- "Yeats and Shakespeare," *Centenary Essays*, ed. Maxwell and Bushrui, pp. 1–17.

-- "W. B. Yeats: *The Second Coming*," *Die Neuren Sprachen*,

I (1961), 301—313.

Kliewer, Warren. "The Bruised Body," *Cresset*, XXXII (1969), 8—12.

Knights, L. C. "Poetry and Social Criticism: The Work of W. B. Yeats," *Explorations* (London, 1946), pp. 170—185.

-- "W. B. Yeats: The Assertion of Values," *Southern Review*, VII (1942), 426—441.

Kohli, Devindra. "Yeats and Eliot: The Magnitude of Contrast? " *Quest*, LVIII (1968), 42—46.

Kostelanetz, Anne. "Irony in Yeats's Byzantine Poems," *Tennessee Studies in Literature*, IX (1964), 129—142.

Krause, David. "The Playwright's Not for Burning," *Virginia Quarterly*, XXXIV (1958), 60—76.

Kuić, Ranka. "Jeitsova l ubavna lirika," *Knizeone Novine*, 355 (June 7, 1969), 3, 12.

Lago, Mary M. "The Parting of the Ways: A Comparative Study of Yeats and Tagore," *A Quarterly of South Asian Literature* (University of Chicago), III (1966), 32—57.

Lakin, R. D. "Unity and Strife in Yeats' Tower Symbol," *Midwest Quarterly*, I (1960), 321—332.

Lapisardi, Frederick S. "The Same Enemy: Notes on Certain Similarities between Yeats and Strindberg," *Modern Drama*, XII (1969), 146—154.

Leach, Elsie. "Yeats's 'A Friend's Illness' and Herbert's 'Vertue,' " *Notes & Queries*, IX (1962), 215.

Leavis, F. R. "The Great Yeats and the Latest," *Scrutiny*, VIII (1940), 437–440.

-- "The Latest Yeats," *Scrutiny*, III (1934), 293–295.

-- "W. B. Yeats," *The Permanence of Yeats*, ed. Hall and Steinmann, pp. 146–159. See also *New Bearings in English Poetry*, pp. 27–50.

Lees, F. N. "Yeats's 'Byzantium,' Dante, and Shelley," *Notes & Queries*, IV (1957), 312–313.

Lerner, Laurence. "W. B. Yeats: Poet and Crank," *Proceedings of the British Academy*, XLIX (1963), 49–67.

Lesser, Simon O. " 'Sailing to Byzantium'--Another Voyage, Another Reading," *College English*, XXVIII (1967), 291–310.

Levin, Gerald. "The Yeats of the *Autobiographies:* A Man of Phase 17," *Texas Studies in Literature and Language*," VI (1965), 398–405.

Levine, Bernard. "A Psychoanalytic Analysis of Yeats's 'Leda and the Swan,' " *Bucknell Review*, XVII (1969), 85–111.

-- " 'High Talk': A Concentrative Analysis of a Poem by Yeats," *James Joyce Quarterly*, III (1966), 124–129.

Lightfoot, Marjorie J. "*Purgatory* and *The Family Reunion:*
In Pursuit of Prosodic Description," *Modern Drama*, VII
(1965), 256–266.

Linebarger, James M. "Yeats's 'Among School Children' and
Shelley's 'Defence of Poetry,' " *Notes & Queries*, X
(1963), 375–377.

Linke, Hansjürgen. "Das Los des Menschen in den Cuchulain
Dramen," *Die Neuren Sprachen*, XIV (1965), 253–268.

Lister, Raymond. "Beulah to Byzantium: A Study of Parallels
in the Works of W. B. Yeats, William Blake, Samuel Palmer,
and Edward Calvert," *Yeats Centenary Papers*, ed. Liam
Miller, pp. 29–68.

Loftus, Richard J. "Yeats and the Easter Rising: A Study in
Ritual," *Arizona Quarterly*, XVI (1960), 168–177.

Lucas, John. "Yeats and Goethe," London *Times Literary
Supplement*, November, 1968, p. 1321.

Mabbott, T. O. "Yeats's 'The Wild Swans at Coole,' " *Ex –
plicator*, III (1944), item 5.

Mackey, William F. "Yeats's Debt to Ronsard on a Carpe Diem
Theme," *Comparative Literature*, XIX (1946), 4–7.

MacLeish, Archibald. "Public Speech and Private Speech in
Poetry," *Yale Review*, XXVII (1938), 536–547. See also
Time to Speak (Boston: Houghton Mifflin, 1940), pp. 59–70.

MacLeod, Fiona (William Sharp). "The Later Work of Mr. Yeats,"

North American Review, CLXXV (1902), 473–485.

Mac Lochlainn, Alf. "An Unrecorded Yeats Item," *The Irish Book*, I (1962), 61–65.

MacNeice, Louis. "Yeats's Epitaph," *New Republic*, CII (June 24, 1940), 862–863.

Madge, Charles. " 'Leda and the Swan,' " London *Times Literary Supplement*, July 20, 1962, p. 532.

Magaw, Malcolm. "Yeats and Keats: The Poetics of Romanticism," *Bucknell Review*, XIII (1965), 87–96.

Maixner, Paul R. "Yeats' *The Folly of Being Comforted*," *Explicator*, XIII (1954), item 1.

Malins, Edward. "Yeats and Music," *Yeats Centenary Papers*, ed. Liam Miller, pp. 481–508.

-- "Yeats and the Easter Rising," *Yeats Centenary Papers*, ed. Liam Miller, pp. 1–28.

Marcus, Philip H. "Possible Sources of Yeats's 'Dhoya,'" *Notes & Queries*, XIV (1967), 383–384.

Marcus, Philip L. "A Fenian Allusion in Yeats," *University Review* (Dublin), IV (1967), 282.

Margolis, Joseph. "Yeats' *Leda and the Swan*," *Explicator*, XIII (1955), item 34.

March, Derick. "The Artist and the Tragic Vision," *Queen's*

A Yeats Bibliography

Quarterly, LXXIV (1967), 104–118.

Martin, C. H. "A Coleridge Reminiscence in Yeats's 'A Prayer for My Daughter, ' " *Notes & Queries*, XII (1965), 258–260.

-- "W. B. Yeats: An Unpublished Letter," *Notes & Queries*, V (1958), 260–261.

Martin, Graham. "Fine Manners, Liberal Speech: A Note on the Public Poetry of W. B. Yeats," *Essays in Criticism*, XI (1961), 40–59.

-- "*The Wild Swans at Coole*," *An Honoured Guest*, ed. Donoghue and Mulryne, pp. 54–72.

Mason, H. A. "Yeats and the English Tradition," *Scrutiny*, V (1937), 449–451.

-- "Yeats and the Irish Movement," *Scrutiny*, V (1936), 330–332.

Masson, D. I. "The 'Musical Form' of Yeats' 'Byzantium,' " *Notes & Queries*, CXCVIII (1952), 400–401.

-- "Word and Sound in Yeats's 'Byzantium,' " *English Literary History*, XX (1953), 136–160.

Matthiessen, F. O. "The Crooked Road," *Southern Review*, VII (1942), 455–470.

-- "Yeats and Four American Poets," *Yale Review*, XXIII (1934), 611–617.

Maxwell, D. E. S. "Swift's Dark Grove: Yeats and the Anglo—
Irish Tradition," *Centenary Essays*, ed. Maxwell and
Bushrui, pp. 18—32.

Mayhew, George. "A Corrected Typescript of Yeats's 'Easter
1916, ' " *Huntington Library Quarterly*, XXVI (1963), 53—71

McAlindon, T. "The Idea of Byzantium in William Morris and W.
B. Yeats," *Modern Philology*, LXIV (1967), 307—319.

-- "Yeats and the English Renaissance," *Publications of the
Modern Language Association*, LXXXII (1967), 157—169.

McHugh, Roger. "Yeats and Irish Politics," *Texas Quarterly*,
V (1962), 90—100.

-- "Yeats's Kind of Twilight," *Tri—Quarterly*, No. 4 (1965),
pp. 126—129.

Melchiori, Giorgio. "La Cupola di Bisanzio," *Paragone*, XI
(1960), No. 128, 41—70.

-- " 'Leda and the Swan': The Genesis of Yeats' Poem,"
English Miscellany, VII (1956), 147—239.

-- "The Moment of Moments," *A Collection of Critical Essays*
ed. Unterecker, pp. 33—36. See also Melchiori's *The Whole
Mystery of Art*, pp. 283—286.

-- "Yeats and Dante," *English Miscellany*, XIX (1968), 153—
179.

-- "Yeats' 'Beast' and the Unicorn: A Study in the Developme of an Image," *Durham University Journal*, XX (1959), 10–23.

Mendel, Sydney. "Yeats' 'Lapis Lazuli,' " *Explicator*, XIX (1961), item 64.

Menon, Narayana. "W. B. Yeats and the Irish Literary Revival," *Indian Literature*, VIII, ii (1965), 12–22.

Mercier, Vivian. "Douglas Hyde's Share in *The Unicorn from the Stars*," *Modern Drama*, VII (1965), 463–465.

-- "In Defense of Yeats as a Dramatist," *Modern Drama*, VIII (1965), 161–166.

-- "Yeats and 'The Fisherman,' " London *Times Literary Supplement*, June 6, 1958, p. 313.

Mazzaro, Jerome L. "Apple Imagery in Yeats: 'The Song of Wandering Aengus,' " *Modern Language Notes*, LXXII (1957), 342–343.

-- "Yeats' 'The Second Coming,' " *Explicator*, XVI (1957), item 6.

Michie, Donald M. "A Man of Genius and a Man of Talent," *Texas Studies in Literature and Language*, VI (1964), 148–154.

Miller, Liam. "The Dun Emer and the Cuala Press," *Essays in Perspective*, ed. Skelton and Saddlemyer, pp. 141–151.

Mills, John G. "W. B. Yeats and Noh," *Japan Quarterly*, II (1955), 496–500.

Miner, Earl Roy. "A Poem by Swift and W. B. Yeats's *Words Upon the Window—Pane*," *Modern Language Notes*, LXXII (1957), 273–275.

Minton, Arthur. "Yeats' *When You Are Old*," *Explicator*, V (1947), item 49.

Mise, Raymond. "Yeats' Crazy Jane Poems," *Paunch*, No. 25, pp. 18–30.

Mizener, Raymond. "The Romanticism of W. B. Yeats," *Southern Review*, VII (1942), 601–623. See also *The Permanence of Yeats*, ed. Hall and Steinmann, pp. 125–145.

Monahan, Michael. "Yeats and Synge," *Nova Hibernia* (New York: Kennerley, 1914), pp. 13–37.

Monroe, Harriet. "Mr. Yeats and the Poetic Drama," *Poetry*, XVI (1920), 32–39.

Montague, John. " 'Under Ben Bulben,' " *Shenandoah*, XVI (1965), 21–24.

Monteiro, George. "Unrecorded Variants in Two Yeats Poems," *Papers of the Bibliographical Society of America*, LX (1966), 367–368.

Moore, Gerald. "The Nō and the Dance Plays of W. B. Yeats," *Japan Quarterly*, VII (1960), 177–187.

Moore, George. "Yeats, Lady Gregory, and Synge," *English Review*, XVI (1913–1914), 167–180, 350–364.

Moore, John R. "An Old Man's Tragedy--Yeats's *Purgatory*," *Moderm Drama*, V (1963), 440–450.

-- "Cold Passion: A Study of *The Herne's Egg*," *Modern Drama*, VII (1965), 287–298.

-- "Cuchulain, Christ, and the Queen of Love: Aspects of Yeatsian Drama," *Tulane Drama Review*, VI (1962), 150–159.

-- "Swan or Goose?," *Sewanee Review*, LXX (1963), 123–133.

-- "The Idea of a Yeats Play," *Centenary Essays*, ed. Maxwell and Bushrui, pp. 154–166.

-- "The Janus Face: Yeats's *Player Queen*," *Sewanee Review*, LXXVI (1968), 608–630.

-- "Yeats as a Last Romantic," *Virginia Quarterly*, XXXVII (1961), 432–449.

Moore, T. Sturge. "Yeats," *English*, II (1939), 273–278.

Morgan, Margery M. "Shaw, Yeats, Nietzsche, and the Religion of Art," *A Quarterly of Drama and Arts of the Theatre*, I (1967), 24–34.

Mortenson, Robert. "Yeats's *Vision* and 'The Two Trees,' " *Studies in Bibliography*, XVII (1964), 220–222.

Munro, John M. "Arthur Symons and W. B. Yeats: The Quest for Compromise," *Dalhousie Review*, XLV (1965), 137–152.

A Yeats Bibliography

Mulryne, J. R. "The *Last Poems*," *An Honoured Guest*, ed. Donoghue and Mulryne, pp. 124–142.

Murphy, Daniel J. "Maud Gonne's *Dawn*," *Shenandoah*, XVI (1965), 63–77.

-- "Yeats and Lady Gregory: A Unique Dramatic Collaboration," *Modern Drama*, VII (1965), 322–328.

Murry, John Middleton. "Mr. Yeats's Swan Song," *The Permanence of Yeats*, ed. Hall and Steinmann, pp. 9–13.

Nathan, Leonard P. "W. B. Yeats's Experiments with an Influence," *Victorian Studies*, VI (1962), 66–74.

Natterstad, J. H. "Yeats' 'The Cap and Bells,' " *Explicator*, XXV (1967), item 75.

Nelick, Frank C. "Yeats, Bullen, and the Irish Drama," *Modern Drama*, I (1958), 196–202.

Newton, Norman. "Yeats as Dramatist: *The Player Queen*," *Essays in Criticism*, VIII (1958), 269–284.

Nielsen, Helge N. " 'The Two Trees' by William Butler Yeats: The Symbolism of the Poem and Its Relation to Northrop Frye's Theory of Apocalyptic and Demonic Imagery," *Orbis Litterarum*, XXIV (1969), 72–76.

Nielsen, Margaret. "A Reading of W. B. Yeats's Poem 'On a Picture of a Black Centaur by Edmund Dulac,' " *Thoth*, IV (1963), 67–73.

Nims, John F. "Yeats and the Careless Muse," *Learners and Discerners: A Newer Criticism* (Charlottesville, Virginia: University of Virginia Press, 1964), ed. Robert Scholes, pp. 31—60.

Nist, John. "In Defense of Yeats," *Arizona Quarterly*, XVIII (1962), 58—65.

Noon, William. "Yeats and the Human Body," *Thought*, XXX (1955), 188—198.

Notopoulos, James A. " 'Sailing to Byzantium,' " *Classical Journal*, XLI (1945), 78—79.

O'Brien, Conor Cruise. "Passion and Cunning: An Essay on the Politics of W. B. Yeats," *In Excited Reverie*, ed. Jeffares and Cross, pp. 207—278.

-- "Yeats and Irish Politics," *Tri—Quarterly*, No. 4 (1965), pp. 91—98.

O'Brien, James H. "Yeats' Dark Night of Self and *The Tower*," *Bucknell Review*, XV, ii (1967), 10—25.

-- "Yeats' Discoveries of Self in 'The Wild Swans at Coole,' " *Colby Library Quarterly*, VIII (1968), 1—13.

-- "Yeats's Search for Unity of Being," *The Personalist*, XLVIII (1967), 361—371.

O'Connor, Frank. "Quarreling with Yeats: A Friendly Recollection," *Esquire*, LXII, vi (1964), 157, 221, 224—225, 232.

-- "The Old Age of a Poet," *The Bell*, I (1941), 7—18.

-- "The Plays and Poetry of W. B. Yeats," *Listener*, XXV, 643 (May 8, 1941), 675—676.

-- "Two Friends: Yeats and A. E.," *Yale Review*, XXIX (1939), 60—88.

O'Driscoll, Robert. " 'Under Ben Bulben,' " London *Times Literary Supplement*, February 18, 1965, p. 132.

O'Faolain, Sean. "AE and WBY," *Virginia Quarterly*, XV (1939), 41—57.

-- "W. B. Yeats," *English Review*, LX (1935), 680—688.

-- "Yeats and the Younger Generation," *Horizon*, V (1942), 43—54.

-- , review. "*Selected Poems, Lyrical and Narrative*. By W. B. Yeats," *Criterion*, IX (1930), 523—528.

Olson, Elder. " 'Sailing to Byzantium': Prolegomena to a Poetics of the Lyric," *The Permanence of Yeats*, ed. Hall and Steinmann, pp. 257—269. See also *The University Review*, VIII (1942), 209—219.

O'Neil, George. "Irish Drama and Irish Views," *American Catholic Quarterly*, XXXVII, 146 (1912), 322—332.

Orel, Harold. "Dramatic Values: Yeats and *The Countess Cathleen*," *Modern Drama*, II (1959), 8—16.

Ower, John. "Yeats' 'News for the Delphic Oracle,' " *Explicator*, XXVIII (1969), item 7.

Parish, John E. "The Tone of Yeats's *After Long Silence*," *Western Humanities Review*, XVI (1962), 377–379.

Parker, J. Stewart. "Yeats' *The Hour–Glass*," *Modern Drama*, X (1968), 356–363.

Parkinson, Thomas. "The Individuality of Yeats," *Pacific Spectator*, VI (1952), 488–499.

-- "The Modernity of Yeats," *Southern Review*, V (1969), 922–934.

-- "The Sun and the Moon in Yeats's Early Poetry," *Modern Philology*, L (1952), 50–58.

-- "The World of Yeats' 'Nineteen–Hundred and Nineteen,' " *English Studies* (University of California), XI (1955), 211–227.

-- "Vestiges of Creation," *Sewanee Review*, LXIX (1961), 80–111.

-- "W. B. Yeats: A Poet's Stagecraft, 1899–1911," *English Literary History*, XVII (1950), 136–161.

-- "Yeats and Pound: The Illusion of Influence," *Comparative Literature*, VI (1954), 256–264.

-- "Yeats and the Love Lyric," *James Joyce Quarterly*, III (1966), 109–123.

Parks, L. C. "The Hidden Aspect of 'Sailing to Byzantium,' "
Études Anglaisses, XVI (1963), 333–344.

Partridge, Edward B. "Yeats's 'The Three Bushes'--Genesis
and Structure," *Accent,* XVII (1957), 67–80.

Patmore, Brigit. "Some Memories of W. B. Yeats," *Texas
Quarterly,* VIII (1965), 152–164.

Peacock, Ronald. "Yeats," *The Poet in the Theatre* (New
York: Harcourt, Brace, 1946), pp. 117–128.

Pearce, Donald R. "Dublin's 'National Literary Society,'
1892," *Notes & Queries,* CXCVI (1951), 213–214.

-- "Flames Begotten of Flame," *Sewanee Review,* LXXIV
(1966), 649–668.

-- "Philosophy and Phantasy: Notes on the Growth of
Yeats's 'System,' " *University of Kansas City Review,*
XVIII (1952), 169–180.

-- "Yeats and the Romantics," *Shenandoah,* VIII (1957), 40–
57.

-- "Yeats's Last Plays: An Interpretation ," *English Literary
History,* XVIII (1951), 67–76.

-- "Yeats's 'The Delphic Oracle upon Plotinus,' " *Notes &
Queries,* I (1954), 175–176.

Pelham, Edgar. "The Enigma of Yeats," *Queen's Quarterly,*
XLVI (1939), 411–422.

A Yeats Bibliography

Perloff, Marjorie. " 'Heart Mysteries': The Later Love Lyrics of W. B. Yeats," *Contemporary Literature*, X (1969), 266–283.

-- "Spatial Form in the Poetry of Yeats: The Two Lissadel Poems," *Publications of the Modern Language Association*, LXXXII (1967), 444–454

-- "The Consolation Theme in Yeats's 'In Memory of Robert Gregory,' " *Modern Language Quarterly*, XXVII (1966), 299–305.

-- "Yeats and the Occasional Poem: 'Easter 1916,' " *Papers on Language and Literature*, IV (1968), 308–328.

Perrine, Laurence. "Yeats' 'An Acre of Grass,' " *Explicator*, XXII (1964), item 64.

Peschmann, Herman. "Yeats and the Poetry of War," *English*, XV (1965), 181–184.

Phillips, Robert S. "Yeats's 'Sailing to Byzantium,' 25–32," *Explicator*, XXII (1963), item 11.

Pirkhofer, A. M. "Zur Bildersprache von Blake und Yeats," *Anglia*, LXXV (1957), 224–233.

Plater, Ormonde. "Water Imagery in Yeats' 'Meditation in Time of Civil War,' " *Style* (University of Arkansas), II (1968), 59–72.

Popkin, Henry. "Yeats as Dramatist," *Tulane Drama Review*, III (1959), 73–82.

Porter, Katherine Anne. "From the Notebooks of Katherine Anne Porter--Yeats, Joyce, Eliot, Pound," *Southern Review*, I (1965), 570–573.

Prior, Moody E. "Yeats's Search for a Dramatic Form," *Tri–Quarterly*, No. 4 (1965), pp. 112–114.

Quinn, Sister M. Bernetta. "Symbolic Landscape in Yeats: County Sligo," *Shenandoah*, XVI (1965), 37–60.

-- "Yeats and Ireland," *English Journal*, LIV (1965), 449–450.

Refroidi, Patrick. "W. B. Yeats: Sligo ou Byzance?," *Les Langues Modernes*, LX (1966), 45–54.

Raine, Kathleen. "A Traditional Language of Symbols," *Listener*, LX (1958), 559–560.

-- "Yeats and Platonism," *Texas Quarterly*, X (1967), 161–181. See also *The Dublin Magazine*, VII, i (1968), 38–63.

-- "Yeats, the Tarot, and the Golden Dawn," *Sewanee Review*, LXXVII (1969), 112–148.

-- "Yeats's Debt to William Blake," *Texas Quarterly*, VIII (1965), 165–181.

Raines, Charles A. "Yeats' Metaphors of Permanence," *Twentieth Century Literature*, V (1959), 12–20.

Rajan, Balachendra. "The Reality Within," *Indian Journal of English Studies*, VI (1965), 44–55.

-- "Yeats and the Absurd," *Tri—Quarterly*, No. 4 (1965), pp. 130–137.

Ram, Alur J. "Yeats and Shakespeare's Tragic Vision," *An English Miscellany* (India), III (1965), 103–118.

-- "Yeats on Shakespeare," *Phoenix* (Korea), XI (1967), 53–71.

Ramamruthan, J. V. "Indian Themes in the Poetry of W. B. Yeats," *The Literary Half—Yearly*, No. 2 (1960), pp. 43–48.

Ransom, John Crowe. "Old Age of a Poet," *Kenyon Review*, II (1940), 345–347.

-- "The Irish, the Gaelic, the Byzantine," *Southern Review*, VII (1942), 517–546.

-- "The Severity of Mr. Savage," *Kenyon Review*, VII (1945), 114–117.

-- "Yeats and His Symbols," *Kenyon Review*, I (1939), 309–322. See also *The Permanence of Yeats*, ed. Hall and Steinmann, pp. 85–96.

Read, Herbert. "The Later Yeats," *A Coat of Many Colors* (London: Routledge, 1945), pp. 208–212.

Reed, Victor. "Yeats' 'High Talk,' " *Explicator*, XXVI (1968), item 52.

Reid, B. L. "The House of Yeats," *Hudson Review*, XVIII

A Yeats Bibliography

(1965), 331–350.

-- "Yeats and Tragedy," *Hudson Review*, XI (1958), 391–410.

Reid, J. D. "Leda, Twice Assaulted," *Journal of Aesthetics and Art Criticism*, XI (1953), 378–389.

Reiman, Donald H. "Yeats's *Deirdre, English Studies*, XLII (1961), 218–232.

Reinert, Otto. "Yeats' *The Hour–Glass*," *Explicator*, XV (1956), item 19.

Rhys, Ernest. "W. B. Yeats: Early Recollections," *Fortnightly Review*, CXXXVIII (July, 1935), 52–57.

Richardson, Dorothy M. "Yeats of Bloomsbury," *Life and Letters To–Day*, XXI (1939), 60–66.

Robinson, Lennox. "The Man and the Dramatist," *Essays in Tribute*, ed. Gwynn, pp. 55–114.

-- "William Butler Yeats: Personality," *In Excited Reverie*, ed. Jeffares and Cross, pp. 14–23.

-- "Yeats: The Early Poems," *Review of English Literature*, VI (1965), 22–33.

Rodgers, R. W. "W. B. Yeats: A Dublin Portrait," *In Excited Reverie*, ed. Jeffares and Cross, pp. 1–13.

Roland, Holst A. "William Butler Yeats Herdacht," *Verslagen en Mededelingen van de Konink lÿke Vlamse Academie voor*

Tool—en Letterkunde, pp. 5—6.

Roll—Hansen, Diderik. "W. B. Yeats some Dramatiker," *Edda*, LII (1965), 153—164.

Rose, Marilyn G. "A Visit with Anne Yeats," *Modern Drama*, VII (1964), 299 307.

-- "The Daughters of Herodias in *Herodiade, Salomé*, and *A Full Moon in March*," *Comparative Drama*, I (1967), 72—181.

Rose, William. "A Letter from W. B. Yeats on Rilke," *German Life and Letters*, XV (1961), 68—70.

Rosenbaum, S. P. "Yeats' 'Among School Children,' " *Explicator*, XXIII (1964), item 14.

Rosenburg, Bruce A. "Irish Folklore and 'The Song of Wandering Aengus,' " *Philological Quarterly*, XLVI (1967), 527—535.

Rosenthal, M. L. "Introduction," *Selected Poems and Two Plays of William Butler Yeats* (New York: Collier Books, 1962), ed. M. L. Rosenthal, xv—xxxix.

-- "On Yeats and the Cultural Symbolism of Modern Poetry," *Yale Review*, XLIX (1960), 573—583.

-- "Sources in Myth and Magic," *Nation*, CLXXXII (1956), 533—535.

Rothenstein, Sir William. "Yeats as a Painter Saw Him,"

Essays in Tribute, ed. Gwynn, pp. 35—54.

Rubenstein, Jerome S. "Three Misprints in Yeats's *Collected Poems*," *Modern Language Notes*, LXX (1955), 184—187.

Russell, George William (AE). "Yeats's Early Poems," *Living Age*, CCCXXVII (November 28, 1925), 464—466.

Rutherford, Andrew. "Yeats' *Who Goes with Fergus?*," *Explicator*, XIII (1955), item 41.

Ruthven, K. K. "Propertius, Wordsworth, Yeats, Pound and Hale," *Notes & Queries*, XV (1968), 47—48.

Rynehart, J. G. "Wilde's Comments on Early Works of W. B. Yeats," *The Irish Book*, I (1962), 102—104.

Saddlemyer, Ann. "Image—Maker for Ireland: Augusta Lady Gregory," *Essays in Perspective*, ed. Skelton and Saddlemyer, pp. 203—222.

-- "The Cult of the Celt: Pan—Celticism in the Nineties," *Essays in Perspective*, pp. 19—21.

-- "The Heroic Discipline of the Looking Glass: W. B. Yeats's Search for Dramatic Design," *Essays in Perspective*, pp. 87—103.

-- "The Noble and the Beggar Man: Yeats and Literary Nationalism," *Essays in Perspective*, pp. 22—39.

-- "Worn out with Dreams: Dublin's Abbey Theatre," *Essays in Perspective*, pp. 104—132.

A Yeats Bibliography

Salerno, Nicholas A. "A Note on Yeats and Leonardo da Vinci," *Twentieth Century Literature*, V (1960), 197–198.

Sandberg, Anna. "The Anti–Theater of W. B. Yeats," *Modern Drama*, IV (1961), 131–137.

Sanders, Paul. "Yeats' 'The Magi,' " *Explicator*, XXV (1967), item 53.

Sanesi, Roberto. " 'Lapis Lazuli,' " *Osservatore Politico Letterario*, VII (1961), 81–91.

-- " 'Lapsus Lazuli' di W. B. Yeats," *Poesia e Critica*, I (1961), 5–18.

-- "William Butler Yeats Uomo Publico," *Aut Aut*, LXVII (1961), 69–71.

Saul, George Brandon. "A Frenzy of Concentration: Yeats's Verse from *Responsibilities* to *The King of the Great Clock Tower*," *Arizona Quarterly*, XX (1964), 101–116.

-- "Coda: The Verse of Yeats's Last Five Years," *Arizona Quarterly*, XVII (1961), 63–68.

-- "In . . . Luminous Wind," *Yeats Centenary Papers*, ed. Liam Miller, pp. 197–256.

-- "Jeffares on Yeats," *Modern Language Notes*, LXVI (1951), 246–249.

-- "The Short Stories of William Butler Yeats," *Poet Lore*, LVII (1962), 371–374.

-- "The Winged Image: A Note on Birds in Yeats's Poems," *Bulletin of the New York Public Library*, LVIII (1954), 267–273.

-- "Thread to a Labyrinth: A Selective Bibliography in Yeats," *Bulletin of the New York Public Library*, LVIII (1954), 344–347.

-- "Yeats and His Poems," London *Times Literary Supplement*, March 31, 1950.

-- "W. B. Yeats: Corrigenda," *Notes & Queries*, VII (1960), 302–303.

-- "Yeats, Noyes, and Day Lewis," *Notes & Queries*, CXCV (1950), 258.

-- "Yeats's Hare," London *Times Literary Supplement*, January 11, 1947, p. 23.

-- "Yeats's Verse Before *Responsibilities*," *Arizona Quarterly*, XVI (1960), 158–167.

-- "Yeatsian Brevities," *Notes & Queries*, I (1954), 535–536.

Savage, D. S. "The Aestheticism of W. B. Yeats," *Kenyon Review* VII (1945), 118–134. See also *The Permanence of Yeats*, ed. Hall and Steinmann, pp. 173–194.

-- "Two Prophetic Poems," *Adelphi*, XXII (October–December, 1945), 25–32.

Scanlon, Sister Aloyse. "The Sustained Metaphor in *The Only*

Jealousy of Emer," *Modern Drama*, VII (1965), 273–277.

Schanzer, Ernest. " 'Sailing to Byzantium,' Keats, and Anderson," *English Studies*, XLI (1960), 376–380.

Schaup, Susanne. "W. B. Yeats: Image of a Poet in Germany," *Southern Humanities Review*, II (1968), 313–323.

Schneidau, Herbert N. "Pound and Yeats: The Question of Sym— bolism," *English Literary History*, XXXII (1965), 220–237.

Schneider, Elisabeth. "Yeats's 'When You Are Old,' " *Explicator*, VI (1948), item 50.

Schramm, Richard. "The Line Unit: Studies in the Later Poetry of W. B. Yeats," *Ohio University Review*, III (1961), 32–41.

Schrickx, W. "On Giordano Bruno, Wilde, and Yeats," *English Studies*, XL (1959), Supplement, 257–264.

-- "William Butler Yeats: Symbolist en Visionair Dirchter," *De Vlaamse Gids*, XLIX (1965), 380–396.

Schroeter, James. "Yeats and the Tragic Tradition," *Southern Review*, I (1965), 835–846.

Schwartz, Delmore. "An Unwritten Book," *Southern Review*, VII (1942), 471–491. See also *The Permanence of Yeats*, ed. Hall and Steinmann, pp. 277–295.

Seiden, Morton L. "A Psychoanalytical Essay on W. B. Yeats," *Accent*, VI (1946), 178–190.

-- "Patterns of Belief: Myth in the Poetry of W. B. Yeats," *American Imago*, V (1948), 258–300.

-- "W. B. Yeats as a Playwright," *Western Humanities Review*, XIII (1959), 83–98.

Sena, Vinod. "W. B. Yeats and English Poetic Drama," *An English Miscellany*, II (1963), 23–36.

-- "W. B. Yeats and the Indian Way of Wisdom," *Quest*, LXII (1969), 76–79.

-- "Yeats on the Possibility of an English Poetic Drama," *Modern Drama*, IX (1966), 195–205.

Seng, Peter J. "Yeats' 'The Folly of Being Comforted,' " *Explicator*, XVII (1959), item 48.

Servotte, Herman. "Van Innisfree naar Byzantium W. B. Yeats (1865–1939)," *Dietsche Warrande en Belfort*, CX (1965), 13–27.

Shanley, J. Lyndon. "Thoreau's Geese and Yeats's Swans," *American Literature*, XXX (1958), 361–364.

Shields, H. E. "Yeats and the 'Sally Gardens,' " *Hermathena*, CI (1965), 22–26. Yeats issue.

Sickels, Eleanor M. "Yeats' 'I am of Ireland,' " *Explicator*, XV (1965), item 10.

-- "Yeats' 'The Gyres,' 6," *Explicator*, XV (1957), item 60.

Sidnell, N. J. "Manuscript Versions of Yeats's *The Shadowy Waters:* An Abbreviated Description and Chronology of the Papers Relating to the Play in the National Library of Ireland," *Papers of the Bibliographical Society.* LXII (1968), 39–57.

-- "Yeats's First Work for the Stage: The Earliest Versions of *The Countess Kathleen,*" *Centenary Essays,* ed. Maxwell and Bushrui, pp. 167–188.

Sitwell, Edith. "William Butler Yeats," *Aspects of Modern Poetry* (London: Duckworth, 1934), pp. 73–89.

Skeffington, Owen S. "W. B. Yeats," London *Times Literary Supplement,* July 8, 1965, p. 579.

Skelton, Robin. "A Literary Theatre: A Note on English Poetic Drama in the Time of Yeats," *Essays in Perspective,* ed. Skelton and Saddlemyer, pp. 133–140.

-- "Division and Unity: AE and W. B. Yeats," *Essays in Perspective,* pp. 223–232.

-- "Images of a Poet: W. B. Yeats," *The Irish Book,* I (1962), 89–97.

-- "The Workshop of W. B. Yeats," *Concerning Poetry,* I (1968), 17–26.

-- "Unarranged Reality: The Paintings and Writings of Jack B. Yeats," *Essays in Perspective,* pp. 254–265.

-- "W. B. Yeats: The Poet as Synopsis," *A Journal for the*

Comparative Study of Literature and Ideas, I (1967), 7—21.

Slattery, Sister Margaret P. *"Deirdre:* The 'Mingling of Con—traries' in Plot and Symbolism," *Modern Drama,* XI (1969), 400—404.

Smith, A. J. M. "A Poet Young and Old--W. B. Yeats," *Toronto Quarterly,* VIII (1939), 309—322.

Smith, Grover. "Yeats's 'Cat and the Moon,' " *Notes & Queries,* CXCV (1950), 35.

Snow, Wilbert. "A Yeats—Longfellow Parallel," *Modern Language Notes,* LXXIV (1959), 302—303.

Southam, B. C. "Life and the Creator in 'The Long—Legged Fly,' *Twentieth Century Literature,* VI (1961), 175—179.

-- "Yeats' 'Long—Legged Fly,' " *Explicator,* XXII (1964), item 73.

Spanos, William V. "Sacramental Imagery in the Middle and Late Poetry of W. B. Yeats," *Texas Studies in Literature and Language,* IV (1962), 214—227.

Spencer, Theodore. "The Later Poetry of W. B. Yeats," *Literary Opinion in America* (New York: Harper, 1938), pp.263 —277.

Spender, Stephen. "La Crise des Symboles," *France Libre,* VII (1943), 206—210.

-- "The Influence of Yeats on Later English Poets," *Tri—Quarterly,* No. 4 (1965), pp. 82—89.

-- "Yeats as a Realist," *The Permanence of Yeats*, ed. Hall and Steinmann, pp. 160–172. See also *Criterion*, XIV, i (1934), 17–26, and Spender's *The Destructive Element*, pp. 115–132.

-- , Patrick Kavanaugh, Thomas Kinsella, and W. B. Snodgrass. "Poetry Since Yeats: An Exchange of Views," *Tri–Quarterly*, No. 4 (1965), pp. 100–111.

Spitzer, Leo. "On Yeats's Poem 'Leda and the Swan,'" *Modern Philology*, LI (1953–1954), 271–276.

Spivak, Gayatri C. "Principles of the Mind: Continuity in Yeats' Poetry," *Modern Language Notes*, LXXXIII (1968), 882–899.

Stageberg, Norman. "Yeats's 'Sailing to Byzantium,'" *Explicator*, VI (1947), item 14.

Stallworthy, Jon. "Two of Yeats's Last Poems," *Review of English Literature*, IV (1963), 48–69.

-- "W. B. Yeats and the Dynastic Theme," *Critical Quarterly*, VII (1965), 247–265.

-- "Yeats as Anthologist," *In Excited Reverie*, ed. Jeffares and Cross, pp. 171–192.

-- "W. B. Yeats's 'Under Ben Bulben,'" *Review of English Studies*, XVII (1966), 30–53.

Stamm, Rudolph. " 'The Sorrows of Love,' A Poem by W. B. Yeats," *English Studies*, XXIX (1948), 78–87.

-- "William Butler Yeats: *Deirdre*," *Das Moderne Englische Drama* (Berlin: Erich Schmidt, 1963), ed. Horst Oppel, pp. 62–86.

-- "W. B. Yeats und Oscar Wilde's 'Ballad of Reading Gaol,' " *Studies in English Language and Literature* (Vienna and Stuttgart: Braumuller, 1958), ed. Siegfried Korninger, pp. 210–219.

Stanford, W. B. "Yeats in the Irish Senate," *Review of English Studies*, IV (1963), 71–80.

Starkie, Walter. "W. B. Yeats and the Abbey Theatre," *Southern Review*, V (1969), 886–921.

Staub, August W. "The 'Unpopular Theatre' of W. B. Yeats," *Quarterly Journal of Speech*, XLVII (1961), 363–371.

-- "Yeats: The Hundredth Year," *Quarterly Journal of Speech*, LII (1966), 81–85.

Stauffer, Donald A. "Artist Shining Through his Vehicles," *Kenyon Review*, XI (1949), 330, 332–334.

-- "The Reading of a Lyric Poem," *Kenyon Review*, XI (1949), 426–440.

-- "Yeats and the Medium of Poetry," *English Literary History*, XV (1948), 227–246.

Stebner, Gerhard. "William Butler Yeats: *The Countess Cathleen*," *Das Moderne Englische Drama*, ed. Horst Oppel, pp. 28–43.

Stein, Arnold. "Yeats: A Study in Recklessness," *Sewanee Review*, LVII (1949), 603–626.

Stemmler, Theodore. "W. B. Yeats' *Song of the Happy Shepherd* und Shelley's *Defence of Poetry*," *Neophilologous*, XLVII (1963), 221–225.

Stevenson, W. H. "Yeats and Blake: The Use of Symbols," *Centenary Essays*, ed. Maxwell and Bushrui, pp. 219–225.

Stock, Amy G. "*A Vision*," *Yeats: A Collection of Critical Essays*, ed. Unterecker, pp. 139–154. See also Stock's *W. B. Yeats: His Poetry and Thought* (Cambridge, 1961), pp. 146–164.

-- "From the National to the Universal," *Dublin Magazine*, IV, iii (1965), 28–35. Yeats issue.

-- "The World of Maud Gonne," *Indian Journal of English Studies*, VI (1965), 56–79.

-- "Yeats and Achebe," *Journal of Commonwealth Literature* (University of Leeds), V (1968), 105–111.

Strong, L. A. G. "William Butler Yeats," *Essays in Tribute*, ed. Gwynn, pp. 183–229.

Stucki, Yasuko. "Yeats's Drama and the Nō: A Comparative Study in Dramatic Methods," *Modern Drama*, IX (1966), 101–122.

Sturtevant, Donald F. "The Public and Private Minds of William Butler Yeats," *Thoth*, IV (1963), 74–82.

A Yeats Bibliography

Sullivan, Ruth E. "Backward to Byzantium," *Literature and Psychology*, XVII (1967), 13–18.

Suss, Irving D. "Yeatsian Drama and the Dying Hero," *South Atlantic Quarterly*, LIV (1955), 369–380.

Symons, Arthur. "Mr. W. B. Yeats," *Studies in Prose and Verse* (New York: Dutton, 1904 (?)), pp. 230–241.

Szladits, Lola L. "Addenda to Sidnell: Yeats's 'The Shadowy Waters,' " *Papers of the Bibliographical Society of America*, LXII (1968), 614–617.

Tate, Allen. "Yeats's Romanticism: Notes and Suggestions," *Southern Review*, VII (1942), 591–600. See also *Yeats: A Collection of Critical Essays*, ed. Unterecker, pp. 155–162, and Tate's *Collected Essays* (Denver: Alan Swallow, 1959).

Taube, Myron. "Yeats' 'An Acre of Grass,' 10," *Explicator*, XXVI (1968), item 40.

Terwilliger, Patricia J. "A Re–Interpretation of Stanzas VII and VIII of W. B. Yeats's 'Among School Children,' " *Boston University Studies in English*, V (1961), 29–34.

Thatcher, David S. "A Misdated Yeats Letter on Nietzsche," *Notes & Queries*, XV (1968), 286–287.

Theumer, Erich. "W. B. Yeats: *Adam's Curse*," *Die Neuren Sprachen*, XVI (1967), 305–310.

Thompson, Francis J. "Poetry and Politics: W. B. Yeats," *Hopkins Review*, III (1950), 3–17.

A Yeats Bibliography

Thompson, J. B. "The Tables Turned: An Analysis of Yeats's
'Crazy Jane Reproved,' " *English Studies in Africa*, XI
(1968), 173–183.

Thwaite, Anthony. "Yeats and the Noh," *Twentieth Century*,
CLXII (1957), 235–242.

Tindall, William York. "The Symbolism of W. B. Yeats,"
Accent, V (1945), 203–212. See also *The Permanence
of Yeats*, ed. Hall and Steinmann, pp. 238–249; *Yeats:
A Collection of Critical Essays*, ed. Unterecker, pp. 43–
53; and Tindall's *Forces in Modern British Literature*
(New York: Knopf, 1947), pp. 248–263.

Tomlin, E. W. F. "The Continuity of Yeats," *Phoenix* (Korea),
X (1965), 60–65. Special Edition.

Tomlinson, Charles. "Yeats and the Practising Poet," *An
Honoured Guest*, ed. Donoghue and Mulryne, pp. 1–7.

Torchiana, Donald T. " 'Among School Children' and the Education of the Irish Spirit," *In Excited Reverie*, ed. Jeffares
and Cross, pp. 123–150.

-- "Some Dublin Afterthoughts," *Tri–Quarterly*, No. 4 (1965),
pp. 138–143.

-- "Senator Yeats, Burke, and Able Men," *Newberry Library
Bulletin*, V (1961), 267–280.

-- "W. B. Yeats, Jonathan Swift, and Liberty," *Modern Philology*, LXI (1963), 26–39.

91

-- , and Glenn O'Malley, ed. "Some New Letters from W. B. Yeats to Lady Gregory," *Review of English Literature* (University of Leeds), IV (1963), 9–47.

Trowbridge, Hoyt. " 'Leda and the Swan': A Longinian Analysis," *Modern Philology*, LI (1953–1954), 118–129.

Tsukimura, Reiko. "A Comparison of Yeats's *At the Hawk's Well* and Its Noh Version, *Taka no izumi*," *Literature East and West*, XI (1967), 385–397.

U–Chang, Kim. "The Embittered Sun: Reality in Yeats's Poetry," *Phoenix* (Korea), X (1965), 66–83. Special Edition.

Unger, Leonard. "Yeats and Milton," *South Atlantic Quarterly*, LXI (1962), 197–212.

Unterecker, John E. "A Fair Chance of a Disturbed Ireland: W. B. Yeats to Mrs. J. Duncan," *Massachusetts Review*, V (1964), 315–322.

-- "An Interview with Anne Yeats," *Shenandoah*, XVI (1965), 7–20.

-- "Introduction," *Yeats: A Collection of Critical Essays*, ed. Unterecker, pp. 1–6.

-- "Yeats and Patrick Mc Carten: A Fenian Friendship," *Yeats Centenary Papers*, ed. Liam Miller, pp. 333–444.

Ure, Peter. "A Source of Yeats's 'Parnell's Funeral,' " *English Studies*, XXXIX (1958), 257–258.

-- "The Evolution of Yeats's *The Countess Cathleen*," *Modern Language Review*, LVII (1962), 12–24.

-- "The Hero on the World Tree: Yeats's Plays," *English*, XV (1965), 169–172.

-- "The Integrity of Yeats," *Cambridge Journal*, III (1949), 80–93.

-- "The Plays," *An Honoured Guest*, ed. Donoghue and Mulryne, pp. 143–164.

-- " 'The Statues': A Note on the Meaning of Yeats's Poem," *Review of English Studies*, XXV (1949), 254–257.

-- "Yeats and the Two Harmonies," *Modern Drama*, VII (1964), 237–255.

-- "Yeats's Christian Mystery Plays," *Review of English Studies*, XI (1960), 171–182.

-- "Yeats's Hero–Fool in *The Herne's Egg*," *Huntington Library Quarterly*, XXIV (1961), 125–136.

-- "Yeats's Supernatural Songs," *Review of English Studies*, VII (1956), 38–51.

Vance, Thomas. "Dante, Yeats, and Unity of Being," *Shenandoah*, XVII (1966), 73–85.

Vendler, Helen. "Assimilating Yeats," *Massachusetts Review*, VII (1966), 590–597.

-- "Yeats's Changing Metaphors for the Other World," *Modern Drama*, VII (1964), 308–321.

Venter, J. A. "Phonic Patterning in 'Sailing to Byzantium,' " *English Studies in Africa*, X (1967), 40–46.

Vestdÿk, S. "Kroniek von de poezie: Nestoriaansche Overpeinzingen," *De Gids*, CXIX (1956), 203–209.

Vickery, John B. "*The Golden Bough* and Modern Poetry," *Journal of Aesthetics and Art Criticism*, XV (1957), 271–288.

-- "Three Modes and a Myth," *Western Humanities Review*, XII (1958), 371–378.

Vogel, Joseph F. "Yeats's 'Nine–and–Fifty' Swans," *English Language Notes*, V (1968), 297–300.

Wade, Allan, ed. "Some Letters from W. B. Yeats to John O'Lear and His Sister, from Originals in the Berg Collection," *Bulletin of the New York Public Library*, LVII (1953), 11–12, 76–87.

Wain, John. "W. B. Yeats: 'Among School Children,' " *Interpretations* (London: Routledge and Kegan Paul, 1955), ed. John Wain, pp. 194–210.

Walcutt, C. C. "Yeats' 'Among School Children, ' v," *Explicator*, XXVI (1968), item 72.

-- "Yeats' *Among School Children* and *Sailing to Byzantium*," *Explicator*, VIII (1950), item 42.

A Yeats Bibliography

Wall, Richard J., and Roger Fitzgerald. "Yeats and Jung: An Ideological Comparison," *Literature and Psychology*, XIII (1963), 44–52.

Walton, Geoffrey. "Yeats's *perne:* Bobbin or Bird?," *Essays in Criticism*, XVI (1966), 255–258.

Warren, Austin. "Religio Poetae," *Southern Review*, VII (1942), 624–638. See also *The Permanence of Yeats*, ed. Hall and Steinmann, pp. 200–212, and Warren's *Rage for Order*, pp. 68–84.

Warschausky, Sidney. "Yeats's Purgatorial Plays," *Modern Drama*, VII (1964), 278–286.

Watkins, Vernon. "W. B. Yeats--the Religious Poet," *Texas Studies in Literature and Language*, III (1962), 475–488.

Watson, Thomas L. "The French Reputation of William Butler Yeats," *Comparative Literature*, XII (1960), 256–262.

Watts, C. T. "A Letter from W. B. Yeats to R. B. Cunninghame Greene," *Review of English Studies*, XVIII (1967), 292–293.

Watts, Harold H. "The Tragic Hero in Eliot and Yeats," *Centennial Review*, XIII (1969), 84–100.

-- "Yeats and Lapsed Mythology," *Renascence*, III (1951), 107–112.

-- "W. B. Yeats: Theology Bitter and Gay," *South Atlantic Quarterly*, XLIX (1950), 359–377.

A Yeats Bibliography

Weeks, Donald. "Image and Idea in Yeats' *The Second Coming*," *Publications of the Modern Language Association*, LXIII (1948), 281–292.

Whalley, G. "Yeats' Quarrel with old Age," *Queen's Quarterly*, LVIII (1951), 497–507.

Whitaker, Thomas R. "The Early Yeats and the Pattern of History," *Publications of the Modern Language Association*, LXXV (1960), 320–328.

-- "The Dialectic of Yeats's Vision of History," *Modern Philology*, LVII (1959), 100–112.

-- "William Butler Yeats: History and the Shaping Joy," *Edwardians and Late Victorians* (New York: Columbia University Press, 1959), ed. Richard Ellmann, pp. 80–105.

-- "Yeats's Alembic," *Sewanee Review*, LXVIII (1960), 576–594.

White, Alison. "Yeats' *Byzantium*, 20, and *Sailing to Byzantium*, 30–32," *Explicator*, XIII (1954), item 8.

Wyngaards, N. "The Shadowy Waters van W. B. Yeats en A. Roland Holst," *Spiegel der Letteren*, VI (1963), 197–209.

Wildi, Max. "The Influence and Poetic Development of W. B. Yeats," *English Studies*, XXXVI (1955), 246–253.

Williams, Melvin G. "Yeats and Christ: A Study in Symbolism," *Renascence*, XX (1968), 174–178, 222.

Wilson, Edmund. "W. B. Yeats," *Axel's Castle*, pp. 26–63. See also *The Permanence of Yeats*, ed. Hall and Steinmann, pp. 14–37.

Wilson, F. A. A. "Yeats and Gerhart Hauptmann," *Southern Review*, I (1965), 69–73.

Wilson, F. A. C. "Patterns in Yeats's Imagery: *The Herne's Egg*," *Modern Philology*, LV (1957), 46–52.

-- "Yeats' 'Parnell's Funeral,' II," *Explicator*, XXVII (1969), item 72.

Wind, Edgar. "Raphael: The Dead Child on a Dolphin," London *Times Literary Supplement*, October 25, 1963, p. 874; November 7, 1963, p. 907; November 21, 1963, p. 956.

Winters, Yvor. "The Poetry of W. B. Yeats," *Twentieth Century Literature*, VI (1960), 3–24.

Witemeyer, Hugh H. "From 'Villain' to 'Visionary': Pound and Yeats on Villon," *Comparative Literature*, XIX (1967), 308–320.

Witt, Marion. "A Competition for Eternity: Yeats's Revisions of his Later Poetry," *Publications of the Modern Language Association*, LXIV (1949), 40–58.

-- "A Note on Yeats and Symons," *Notes & Queries*, VII (1960), 467–469.

-- "An Unknown Yeats Poem," *Modern Language Notes*, LXX (1955), 26.

A Yeats Bibliography

-- " 'Great Art Beaten Down': Yeats on Censorship," *College English*, XIII (1952), 248–258.

-- "The Making of an Elegy," *Modern Philology*, XLVIII (1950) 112–121.

-- "Yeats: 1865–1965," *Publications of the Modern Language Association*, LXXX (1965), 311–320.

-- "W. B. Yeats," London *Times Literary Supplement*, April 11, 1952, p. 251.

-- "Yeats on the Poet Laureateship," *Modern Language Notes* LXVI (1950), 385–388.

-- "Yeats to *His Heart, Bidding It Have No Fear*," *Explicator* IX (1951), item 32.

-- "Yeats' *A Dialogue of Self and Soul*," *Explicator*, V (1946) item 48.

-- "Yeats' *The Collar Bone of a Hare*," *Explicator*, VII (1948) item 21.

-- "Yeats' Hare," London *Times Literary Supplement*, Octobe 18, 1947, p. 535.

-- "Yeats' *Mohini Chatterjee, Explicator*, VII (1948), item 21.

-- "Yeats' *Mohini Chatterjee*," *Explicator*, IV (1945), item 60

-- "Yeats' *The Moods*," *Explicator*, VI (1947), item 15.

-- "Yeats's 'The Song of the Happy Shepherd,' " *Philological Quarterly*, XXXII (1953), 1–8.

-- "Yeats' *The Wild Swans at Coole*," *Explicator*, III (1944), item 17.

-- "Yeats' *When You Are Old*," *Explicator*, VI (1947), item 6.

Worth, Katharine J. "Yeats and the French Drama," *Modern Drama*, VIII (1965), 382–391.

Yeats, Michael. "W. B. Yeats and Irish Folk Song," *Southern Folklore Quarterly*, XXXI (1966), 153–178.

-- "Yeats the Public Man," *Southern Review*, V (1969), 872–885.

Yeats, W. B. "The Poetry of Sir Samuel Ferguson," *Dublin University Review*, II (March, 1886), 923–941.

-- "Willie Yeats and John O'Leary," *The Irish Book Lover*, XXVII (November, 1940), 248. While the article is unsigned, Ellmann attributes the spelling in the letter to Yeats.

Youngblood, Sarah. "A Reading of *The Tower*," *Twentieth Century Literature*, V (1959), 74–84.

-- "The Structure of Yeats's Long Poems," *Criticism*, V (1963), 323–335.

Zabel, Morton D. "The Thinking of the Body: Yeats in the *Auto-biographies*," *Southern Review*, VII (1942), 562–590.

-- "Yeats: The Book and the Image," *The Permanence of Yeats*, ed. Hall and Steinmann, pp. 315–326.

Zimmerman, Georges–Denis. "Yeats, the Popular Ballad and the Ballad–Singers," *English Studies*, L (1969), 585–597.

Zwerdling, Alex. "W. B. Yeats: Variations on the Visionary Quest," *Toronto Quarterly*, XXX (1960), 72–85. See also *Yeats: A Collection of Critical Essays*, ed. Unterecker, pp. 80–92.